the

boy

changed

into

a stag

FERENC JUHÁSZ

# Ferenc Juhász

# *the*

# *boy*

# *changed*

# *into*

# *a stag*

## SELECTED POEMS 1949-1967

*Translated by Kenneth McRobbie & Ilona Duczynska*

Toronto New York London
OXFORD UNIVERSITY PRESS
1970

Publication of this book was assisted by the Canada Council.

Printed in Hungary by
Egyetemi Nyomda
(University Printing House)

*This volume is dedicated*

*to the memory of Karl Polanyi,*

*its moving spirit*

# Contents

# Introduction

Ferenc Juhász has long been recognized as a leading figure among the
younger generation of poets in Hungary, and he is now fast achieving an
international reputation.[1] This volume contains English versions of a se-
lection of his poems, including 'The Boy Changed into a Stag Cries Out
at the Gate of Secrets', which Mr W. H. Auden has called 'one of the
greatest poems written in my time'.[2] When he was only twenty-two Juhász
won the highest state award, the Kossuth Prize. *The Breeding Country :
Collected Poems*,[3] a volume of 720 pages, appeared when he was twenty-
nine; 2000 copies were printed soon after the 1956 revolution and these
sold out within three days. Over the years Juhász's work has been the
subject of a great number of critical studies, essays, and reviews. And for
more than a decade some of Hungary's leading critics have suggested that
his work is in the great tradition of Hungarian poetry, along with that of
Sándor Petőfi (1825–49), János Arany (1817–82), Endre Ady (1877–1919),
Attila József (1905–37), Hungary's greatest modern lyric poet with whom

[1] Extracts from the long poems appear in *Ferenc Juhász. Gedichte* (Hamburg: edi-
tions suhrkamp, 1966). In addition to volumes in English and German, individual
poems by Juhász have been translated into Bulgarian, French, Polish, Rumanian,
and Russian.
[2] In *The Plough and the Pen. Writings from Hungary 1930–1956*, edited by Ilona
Duczynska and Karl Polanyi, foreword by W. H. Auden, page 11 (London: Peter
Owen, and Toronto: McClelland & Stewart, 1963); reprinted in *The Penguin
Book of Modern Verse Translation*, edited by George Steiner (London: Penguin,
1966).
[3] Titles are given in English for convenience. A complete list of Juhász's works,
with Hungarian titles, will be found on page 159.

Juhász feels a special kinship, and the most eminent living Hungarian poet, Gyula Illyés (b.1902). In a key article entitled 'Ferenc Juhász, the Renewer' (*Kritika*, October 1966), András Diószegi places the poet within an even more far-reaching tradition.

*His poetry is the fantastically rich summation of fact and idea, concrete objects and symbols, realities and mythologies. He is on the point of creating a poetic image of the world which will be a mirror image of wholeness, and a poetic reality which will be the model of wholeness. What is evoked here is the achievement of ancestors who have summed up in its totality the world-image of Antiquity and the Middle Ages—Lucretius and Dante. And the modern Summers-up : Ady, Bartók and Attila József.*

The Hungarian poetic tradition is made up of great individualists. What the great names that compose it have in common—Juhász among them—is a profound originality coupled with an almost equal talent for generating controversy. For not all critics have been favourable to Juhász. Particularly at certain periods the poet has been a controversial and somewhat isolated figure: as one critic has pointed out, no poet in recent times has been received with so much love and so much hate. These are strong terms, comprehensible only perhaps within the close-knit literary environment of Hungary. But they are also of course an index of the poet's stature and of the challenge implicit in his range, choice of themes, and great originality.

In small countries writers are particularly aware that literature is and remains essentially national. There the uniqueness and limitations of language are more apparent, particularly in Hungary whose tongue is alien to the great language groups of Europe. Also, small nations are vulnerable in politico-cultural relationships with the great. Thus in East Europe for over a century it has fallen to writers and intellectuals to express a heightened sense of nationhood in the name of national survival, and to concern themselves with their country's political, social, and moral welfare. The great Hungarian poet whose life showed this supreme concern was Sándor

Petőfi (Juhász's earliest model) who, at the age of twenty-six, took a leading part in the 1848 revolution and was killed by Austrian and Russian forces in the following year on the battlefield at Segesvár.

In our time this traditional *engagement* is being modified in the countries of Eastern Europe in two ways. First there is the eastwards orientation represented mainly by official opinion that emphasizes the post-1945 ideological ties among east-bloc nations, and that denounces as reactionary whatever it chooses to call 'nationalist' expression in literature. As we shall see, Juhász's poetry is indeed traditional and national in its use of folk forms and themes, and also in its many concrete local and historical allusions and images. It is against these, which some critics have quite wrongly termed obsessions, that hostile criticism has in some measure been directed. Certainly ideological considerations in literature seem not to interest Juhász at all, although he is a convinced communist and humanist. Juhász's earlier poetry frankly hailed the beginnings of socialism in Hungary in 1945. His first volume, *The Winged Colt* (1949), was called healthily revolutionary, and *The Sántha Family* (1950) describes the social transformation of the countryside. However, his poem 'At Twenty-Six' (the age at which Petőfi died) is a wholly personal lyric. And it is rather Juhász's determined humanism that sounds the anti-religious note that runs through his indictment of the old capitalist order that he sees represented by the tombs and sculptured monuments of the Kerepes Cemetery in Budapest (in his poem 'The Grave of Attila József'). Juhász remarked recently on what poetry is *not*: not verbal coitus on the one hand, nor on the other a public hand writing poems against the Americans in Vietnam from what one hears on the radio.

A second challenge to a national focus in poetry in East European countries comes from a growing westward orientation that looks towards artistic experimentation in the widest possible supra-national sense. This is not quite new. For a long time in Hungary the works of highly individual writers like Ady showed distinctive foreign influences, particularly French. And for his part, through travel and extensive reading, Juhász has always kept in touch with developments in the arts abroad: for instance, in recent years he has made a special study of the poetry and life of Dylan Thomas. Nevertheless English-speaking readers will certainly find Juhász's poetry less familiar than that of other modern Hungarian poets—especially his use of traditional forms, his richness of content, and the discursive exoticism of parts of the long poems. Now some official encouragement is being given in Hungary to certain 'safely incomprehensible' forms of avant-garde expression—at the expense, it has been said, of the more traditional emphasis upon content. By contrast, there is so much 'in' Juhász's poetry. His myth-creating genius working within a unique poetic universe, his blazing individualism and profound self-analysis, are expressed in loosely structured yet strongly intellectual and surrealistic images that push subjectivity far beyond mere formal experimentation. It is no surprise that in Hungary he has been called overly modern, a term that when used critically almost always refers to explicit features of content or tone. Several thousand hostile letters were received by the journal that first published Juhász's poem 'The Grave of Attila József'. These made it plain that bigoted Church as well as Party sensibilities were reacting in shock to one image in the opening invocation to the dead poet

*. . . my Ancestor, my Father, my Jesus-genitalled very | own dead . . .*

an image surely of great poetic tenderness.

There have been two periods of hostile criticism. During the early 1950s, Juhász was under great pressure to bring his work into conformity with prevailing canons. A standard reference work published recently now suggests that this criticism was unwarranted, and goes on to observe that as a result Juhász lost his early optimism and turned in upon himself. Nevertheless, during that period his work had continued to be published. But after 1957, when the poet's changed attitude was made the excuse for regarding him not as a more mature talent but as a failure, nothing of his was published in book form until 1965.

Ferenc Juhász was born into an impoverished family of purely peasant background in 1928 in Bia, a village near Budapest, where he lived until he was twenty. A hated period at business school served one useful purpose: to introduce him to science and technology, which as a source of imagery is second only to his inexhaustible store of boyhood memories of village and country life. In the autumn of 1944 he fled from Budapest to avoid conscription just before the terrible siege 'that Christmas written all over with signal rockets'. Years of personal crisis followed, as Juhász frankly tells us in the autobiographical prose poem 'Brief Confessions About Myself' ('One thing obsessed me: suicide'), and other poems continue to tell of recurring despair. Then he began to find himself in new interests. Evenings 'whose flames burned long into the dawn' were spent reading. Already poetry was becoming his main concern, and he began to accumulate the two suitcases-full of 'verse-ruins', which later on he decided to burn. In 1947 Juhász enrolled in literature in one of the People's Colleges, where he was to stay a mere two and a half months. On his first day there he met his future wife: they married almost at once. He met too the 'dear, rock-steady' László Nagy, his friend still—the two are now regarded as the leading figures in the newer contemporary poetry. In 1947 also two poems of his appeared in print, and his first book published in 1949 was to be followed by seven more within ten years. In 1950 he received the Kossuth Prize, the year of the publication of *My Father*, the year too of the death of his beloved father who appears in so many of his poems. His *The Breeding Country: Collected Poems* (1957) was authoritative confirmation of this first richly productive decade, and it has more recently been followed by *Battling the White Lamb* (1965) and *The Flowering World Tree: Selected Poems* (1965), which reveal new dimensions of the poet's talent and sensibility. *What the Poet Can Do*, Juhász's collected prose writings, appeared in 1967. Two years later, a new 460-page volume of verse was published *(Legends of the Holy Flood of Fire)*. Juhász is able to support himself largely by writing, but he also works as a reader for a leading publishing house and until recently was art editor for the literary monthly *Új*

*Írás* (New Writing). He has travelled widely, visiting England, France, the USSR, and several other countries.

Juhász's rich and complex poetry may perhaps best be introduced by singling out one overarching theme within which are several more personal ones: namely, the poet's subtly modulated sense of community, which takes in man, nature, and art. This theme is expressed through strikingly original images of great concreteness and variety on both an intimate and a cosmic scale. First, the community of man is represented in the most personal sense by what Juhász calls 'the bushy foliaged tree of my relatives'. The many receding branches of the family's vanished generations have existence now only through his imagination. This component of heightened consciousness—a recurring motif and article of faith as we shall see—defeats time through its ability to give new reality and meaning to things past. Of all his relations the figures of his parents play a dominant part in Juhász's poetry. The impression of casual grace of the enlarged photographs of them when young, which the poet keeps in his apartment on the Hill of Roses in Buda, is counterbalanced by their later sufferings described in many of his poems. For they appear in almost cruelly sharp focus unblurred by sentiment. When Juhász speaks of himself it is often in terms of his confused feelings for his parents: how as a boy he was conscious of his sense of separateness and guilt, pride and restless searching. Now only his mother is still living. She is shown in several poems as a girl doing labouring jobs and as a young widow taking in laundry; she dominates 'The Boy Changed into a Stag' in which she represents home and the past, and she finds a place too in the most recent poems.

It is Juhász's father whose presence is most strongly felt with a wealth of lovingly observed detail perhaps unique in literature. Images of great beauty and freshness depict incidents from his life, particularly from his last years of gentle acceptance and death. For shortly after Juhász was born, his father, who was also named Ferenc, developed consumption. The obsessive image of the lung occurs in many poems: as cellophane-wrapped rosebushes, the shadow of lace-curtains on a bedroom wall, the bellows of his father's accordion; and Juhász tells how, when lying close to his sleeping father at night, he could hear a rattling like an old dry forest from within the back's scarred trough that was 'the living grave of my childhood'. His father's death forms the climax of 'The Boy Changed into a Stag' and re-echoes in the recurrent death theme in so many other poems. But in the poet's eyes death gave and continues to give to his father a new reality.

Juhász's poetry suggests that awareness of death is an experiencing at a higher power. Death penetrated the family circle so many times with its sounds, its colours, its associations: a bird-call sounding down the chimney, a pair of boots collapsing in the cupboard, candles guttering on graves, wreaths falling apart in the rain. All those lives from the past summoned up in Juhász's poems are seen to be closest to the present at the precise point of their individual deaths. Death is shown as a linking and almost as a positive force. 'At Childhood's Table' opens with death—that 'she' who sat at 'my childhood's flowered oilcloth table'—and closes with the description of the poet returning home and sitting down at the table with those among whom he grew up. Death is shown as a beginning even, making possible for the poet that dialogue which more than anything he seeks with those who gave him life, but who in life maintained a proud and awkward silence. Death is the key to the future, framing a question to which possible answers are without number and without contradiction. From where he lay in his coffin, Juhász writes, his father 'fired gold questions into my tearless eyes'. The genealogy of mortality widens when, visiting his village's graveyard, the poet addresses his father, his ancestors, and all the world's dead, asking 'What did they know of the future?' His relatives cluster in the 'Memory Tree in the love-sown tiny graveyard', which is almost a second home. And of this home's everlasting expectancy, Juhász declares 'I believe in death and I do not believe in annihilation.'

Juhász can say that he does not believe in annihilation because he sees indestructible matter as life's guardian, and, more important, human life's ultimate meaning and preservation in the greater community of society. The poet's memories of life at home in the countryside are recaptured in images that convey the rhythms and forms of existence that are still a dominant feature of Hungarian society. Yet nostalgia has no place. Some of Juhász's descriptions, together with his commentary, have a painful rawness and cruel accuracy, even going so far as to express hatred for the village where life had seemed so confining. In 'The Boy Changed into a Stag' the boy answers his mother's despairing summons, saying that he 'cannot go back' to the old home, that he can drink 'only from a clean spring'. This spring represents no vision of arcadia. For 'the Gate of Secrets', the second part of the poem's title, opens a perspective on another society, the world of work awaiting new generations in the cities:

> each vertebra is a teeming metropolis, for a spleen I have
> a smoke-puffing barge,
> each of my cells is a factory, my atoms are solar systems

There, through his inventive and productive genius, man's handiwork will outlive man; man's nature, rather than the mere beauties of inanimate nature, is the poet's inspiration.

Juhász's second sense of community, with nature, is vivid and distinctive. For him nature is the sub-structure of the human community. Nature is given, has already been created, and is the stage for the drama of what *is being* created from and with her by man. Man must work: that is his nature, and that is the imperative of existence and of value. Not only does work reveal value; its instruments of science and technology that man has fashioned from natural forces may extend his powers *and* his vision. They are the means of understanding as well as of undertaking, and they take their place in a world that Juhász declares is made and has meaning only for man. And nature can accommodate these man-made forms of her forces, as the poet shows in 'Song of the Tractor' where all the horses kneel down to the new machine that has come to share the farm with them. Nature too is shown to be at work, particularly in Juhász's longer poems. Sensuous, infinitely varied, boundless—nature hums and glistens in the poet's conceptualized universe through which man's painfully slow ascent to a unique place is due to his gift of consciousness.

Threatening this consciousness, at the extremes of scale—at the opposing points of the world's pre-history and present-day man's most secret drives—are the nightmare beasts by which Juhász represents nature's predators and human self-destructiveness. For man too is a part of this blind, torrential nature whose directionless energy is like a 'tremendous summer madness throbbing'. Yet in the poem 'Power of the Flowers', the poet asserts that man, a talking flower, possesses a higher beauty through awareness of humankind's community. Only there may the precious fruits of 'purity, goodness, liberty' be preserved, together with humility, watchfulness, and a sense of wholeness. Only there shall man and these qualities 'not burn up apart' like flowers, like 'firelilies in the night'.

In Juhász's poetry consciousness of community is nothing less than individualism raised to its highest power. This leads not to abstraction or subjectivism but to an inner awareness. Thought is sometimes an isolating, a bitter process, as the poet declares in his explicitly titled 'Man Imposes His Pattern upon a Dream': 'When all's said, man decides alone.' The poem ends on the characteristically defiant note

*Wine and soda-water stand upon*
*my table. I take no absolution.*

But neither this nor indeed any of Juhász's poems conveys a total impression of aloneness. Love is the strongest and most immediate impulse towards others. And this is most explicit in those poems in which Juhász refers to his wife Erzsike, that 'wonderful girl-child ... Erzsébet Szeverényi', whom he glimpsed as she was standing at the top of the staircase on his first day in college. She appears beside him, soon to bear their child, at Attila József's graveside, and in many other poems she accompanies the poet into new levels of feeling and self-knowledge. The short poem 'Seasons' tells of her tragic breakdown amid personal and indeed social crisis in 1957; and the strange verse sequence 'Four Voices', with its moral questioning, describes her struggle with death the tempter seen as a white lamb. Her presence is most perfectly evoked through the simplicity and innocent directness of folk ballad.

One can appreciate the puzzled charges of pessimism that have been levelled against Juhász from some quarters in Hungary. His recurring theme of evolving consciousness is on the whole a sombre vision. Life takes place, he seems to be saying, along a frontier beyond which press forces of incoherence and meaninglessness. Fulfilment, even the most personal joy of love, is all too often in the future. Joy may exist, but only as the celebration of past suffering—suffering that is never gratuitous or meaningless, however. It can be 'cleansing', and consciousness can be its long-lasting fruit. Consciousness makes for freedom, and the poet has said that freedom is more important to him than life itself. This is his faith—and faith in faith—which he expresses in the very personal and tender image

*my faith is my dog, back and forth nuzzling the flanks of things with a bark, and atoms, the straggling herd of parts, rustle into a whole again*

['Four Voices']

Thirdly there is the community of art, of all Hungarian writers past and present who form the second family to which Ferenc Juhász so clearly feels he belongs. Poetry had seemed to separate him from his first family. For in 'Brief Confessions about Myself' Juhász describes how his father, when presented with a copy of his son's first book, was alarmed at his choice of career, since to him being a poet meant 'misery and starving to death'. In perhaps the most moving of his longer poems, Juhász describes his visit to the grave of Attila József in the great Kerepes Cemetery in Pest—József, the founder of contemporary Hungarian lyric poetry, the first and most proudly proletarian poet, whom Juhász calls 'First Writing,

2

First Symbol' and 'my Master . . . my Father'. The richly suggestive—and incidentally somewhat disputed—refrain of the first section, 'For you lie here on the other side of the road', may refer to Attila József's suicide in 1937, to his communism, even to his several reburials, for he lies now just outside the Mausoleum of the Heroes of Communism some distance from the graves of his eleven fellow-writers whom Juhász also invokes in the poem. But the line may also refer to his vocation as poet. For Juhász conceives of the poet, as the contents and title of his prose collection indicate, as a man born for a second time into a new relationship with society. For Juhász, poetry is destiny; it is consciousness objectivized, exteriorized, and given permanence through form. Thus József is addressed as 'Spontaneous Pronouncer of the World'. And in his poem 'Images of the Night', Juhász shows the figure of the poet surviving and rebuilding life on an earth that has suffered nuclear destruction and on which his presence is the more necessary,

*for the heart of the Universe shall break when the song ceases.*

\* \* \*

Translation provides a key not only to what had hitherto been inaccessible in terms of language, but to new areas of thought and feeling. It poses special problems of meaning and allusion in rendering poetry that go beyond the technical difficulties of the two languages involved. In recent years, highly regarded translations from comparatively little-known languages have employed the technique used in this volume—dual translation, in which a writer produces versions from texts and notes supplied by a translator whose mother-tongue is that of the original. Accordingly I wish to acknowledge the insight and patience of Ilona Duczynska and her husband Karl Polanyi (1886—1964), dear friends to whom I have been greatly indebted over the last ten years, and the helpfulness of János Miska, who drew my attention to the Hungarian originals of 'Brief Confessions about

Myself' and 'At Childhood's Table' and first drafted them into English for me. And I have tried to incorporate something of what, during the course of several visits to Hungary, I have come to know personally of the poet's attitude to his work.

Thomas Mann once said that even an unsatisfactory rendering of a foreign masterpiece can become a major literary experience. This raises, if perhaps inevitably in somewhat negative terms, the question of quality and also of method. Free translation proves most acceptable only where a well-known poet is privileged to produce a virtually new poem from an original that is usually no longer protected by copyright. However, as working principles free imitation as well as paraphrase were rejected here in the belief that English-speaking readers will wish to be presented as far as possible with the authentic voice of Ferenc Juhász. Every effort has been made, therefore, to convey the tensions, tone, sound, and imagery of the original poems, and above all the formal structure that sustains and shapes Juhász's more exuberant passages and emphasizes the beauty of the simpler poems. The closer the reader can be brought to the work of Ferenc Juhász, the greater will be his impression of a unique poetic universe which—echoing the words of another son of a small country, George Seferis[1]—is on such a scale as to prove that

*In Poetry there are neither big nations nor small.*

KENNETH McROBBIE

[1] In his Nobel Prize for Literature acceptance speech, 1963.

2*

# Acknowledgements

The translators wish to express their gratitude for being able to include in this volume versions of some of the poems of Ferenc Juhász rendered into English by Margaret Avison ('Farm, at Dark, on the Great Plain'), Louis Dudek ('The Foaling Time'), and A.J.M. Smith ('Song of the Tractor' and 'At Twenty-six'). These first appeared, with, 'Man Imposes His Pattern upon a Dream', 'Seasons', and 'The Boy Changed into a Stag Cries Out at the Gate of Secrets', in *The Plough and the Pen: Writings from Hungary 1930—1956* (London and Toronto, 1963). 'The Grave of Attila József' first appeared in *Arion 2* (Budapest, 1968).

Each poem is followed by its date of completion, which in most cases is also that of its first appearance in periodical form.

# Brief
# confessions
# about
# myself

Of my grandparents, only my grandmother on my mother's side is still living: Mrs János Andresz, widow, seventy-six years of age, my bright-eyed, ever curious, gay grandmother, who to this day has kept her soul and her feet healthy running here and there, hoeing the vineyard, going to funerals, nagging her daughter my mother, grumbling at the silences of one by nature more meditative, more stern, of a stricter moral sense and more profound inner life than herself. She does not look at all kindly upon my mother's widowed state, would be happy in fact to see some vigorous, hearty man come along to fire her obstinate, majestic aloofness; although truly she too had been very fond of my father (and that because of his serenity of spirit), and herself had been a young widow, standing with her four children beside the coffin crying for my grandfather, who caught a cold somewhere during the Great War, and after getting back in about his thirty-ninth year died of the war at home; she never so much as thought of another man and didn't remarry. Her nose is hooked; her face's loose fabric gathers in tendril wrinkles, curved chin prominent in relief as on a coin; her temples are white hollows, and with blue eyes blinking out of puckered, brown-speckled leather purse-sockets, she is remarkably like portraits of Goethe at the last—which after all is not that strange, for her ancestors were Swabians. According to her, they migrated from the Black Forest a long time ago and settled here.

I know almost nothing about my forefathers, and my grandmother's recollections are just as limited. Maybe she just doesn't talk of them, or doesn't really remember much beyond a few incidents by now frozen snapshot-like, a few people of interest, some human qualities; it is hard to tell just how much she has jumbled up life as it once was, and girlhood memories; it may also be that what was remembered had already become confused before being passed on to her by her father, who was a shoemaker, or by her mother, of whom so far she has never said a word. People like my grandmother, her parents, and those before them, live out their lives in the present, hoping at most for their descendents' good fortune, for their grandchildren to have a better life, and they tend to think of the future rather than the past. As a result, the past (all those who came before them, and their predecessors in turn) is forgotten in the round of work, and it is only on festive occasions, at times of deep emotion such as births and deaths, that the tattered faces of fathers and great-grandfathers surface like reed roots at low water, like sedge-covered old poplar stumps. And so I, one of thirteen grandchildren and great-grandchildren, share in bringing the myth to birth. Some of my ancestors, lonely islands, loom out of swirling haze; others sink beneath the surface, there is no train of consciousness to hold them, and I can only supplement my family's stories by my imagination howsoever I please: no use cross-questioning the dead.

There were no written family records. Oral tradition's capillaries spread over only a very thin layer of the past. Most even of these had shrivelled with calcifying time, and the clasp-bound German Bible, that sort of old history book rather, contains little more than a few ill-written dates and names. I don't imagine my ancestors were great heroes, taking part or suffering in famous exploits; they could only have been common soldiers, taxpayers, living out their lives along with the rest of the village, their neighbours and relatives, and a generation after their death even their names had faded, sunken in like their graves bearded with the hemlocks and thorns of a new present. But it is of some interest to learn, as I did the other day, that my great-grandparents were generally regarded as prosperous peasants, except for relatives on my father's and his father's side, the Juhász family, who were consistently poor. On the other side, the ancestors of the Steinhausers, Andreszes, and Gallinases were far from badly off, and yet the grandfathers and grandmothers were already landless and penniless day-labourers. It's my belief that even the great-grandparents had slithered into poverty, moulted their fine feathers, in the last years of their lives, and I am increasingly certain that it was not in actual fact economic conditions that made them poor; I believe it was often laziness or daydreaming that wrenched off here and there a piece of their land, crumbling it to smoke-dust. At least that seems to have been the case with grandfather Andresz's father, who sold off quite a few acres of land on the quiet without his wife's knowledge and then spent the money on books, stowing away half of them in the attic and the rest near their maize field under a bridge, in a cavity made by removing a stone in one of its arches. From then on he spent his time reading, mostly in the attic or in the maize field. It was during the course of improving his mind thus that the ruse came to light. His wife, wondering why it was taking him almost three weeks to finish hoeing that half-acre of maize, stole after him and surprised the old fellow stretched out on his stomach under the flowering cherry-tree, greasy hat pulled down over his forehead, smoking his pipe, totally absorbed in the pleasures afforded the mind by an encyclopaedia.

I must confess that just as I have never thought much about my having a mixture of Hungarian, Swabian, and Italian blood in me, I am not particularly interested in whether my forbears, their origins the more strongly leafing out into the past, were well-to-do or not, but rather in whether their occasional acquisition of property came through saving up over a long period or through one of them adding to his lands in a sudden burst of enterprise. Grandfather Juhász was a railway worker—a platelayer or a brakeman, I don't know which—and stocky, bushy moustached, an angry man. Grandfather Andresz was a day-labourer, of medium height, a long black wire moustache growing horizontally straight out from his oval face—his beautiful face, so understanding, with rather sad eyes, the arch of his shaggy mane-like brows supporting the straight forehead's wall; over that thoughtful brow lies black soft waving hair, parted at the side. I know him only from photographs and a suggestion of his memory-face that at times flits across the face of uncle Jani, my mother's brother. He begot five children; he used to be the congregational school supervisor, honorary clerk of the savings bank because he could write a clear hand, and he worked the vineyard of Schulteisz the grocer. In fact it was from the grocery store that he left for America, flew away from the counter-top (they were sitting there drinking brandy on credit) without his wife knowing about it until the letter came from New York asking her to come and join him there with the children. But his wife refused to risk it, and he, having failed to set himself up with a factory out of what he made by washing dishes, came back after a year or two, as poor as when he had gone, painting the boat for his fare across the ocean back to Europe.

My mother's maiden name was Borbála Andresz. A third child, at a very early age she became a maid to one of her aunts, a pretty miserly aunt who was supposed to be the poor little orphan's foster mother. And how insulted she felt when the young girl ran away, felt really humiliated perhaps in her assumed motherliness. Boriska then worked in different places before she got married: in a sack factory, while still quite young I suppose, for she used to tell me long ago that in the midday break she would tussle with the other girls on top of the sack piles; afterwards she worked in a chocolate factory, carried bricks and mortar on building sites, and was a maid in the household of a Jewish lawyer in the years immediately prior to her marriage. My father, the late Ferenc Juhász, had been apprentice bricklayer and became a journeyman; but shortly after his marriage, around when I was born in 1928, he developed consumption, and as the disease got a hold on his system he had to find other less exhausting work for his body transfigured by unceasing fever, work less likely to cause lung haemorrhage, so he took a job as office-messenger with a company called Budanil Ltd, the Hungarian subsidiary of I. G. Farben, I think. My father had a wonderful Tyrolean accordion: its keyboard (eyelid clinging to empty eyehole) was studded with brass flowers; its bellows a fanning peacock's tail, puffed up with love like a blissful termite mother, a leather lung with flower-engraved brass trim—elaborately pleated leather, caterpillar-like, its creases' folds with stitched edgings of fine yellow porous leather like unfledged sparrows' beaks. My grandfather had brought the accordion home from his soldiering for Franz Josef. My father could play it beautifully, sitting during the evenings and on Sundays under the tall mulberry tree, and probably due to that accordion my father contracted tuberculosis. For what is there to do, having an instrument like that and no money, but join a band to bring good cheer to folk at weddings and fairs for an honest copper? And get drunk on that armful's leather-metal throat's vocal cords, on its shrill-low whistlings, on wine, then collapse one winter dawn, soft snow piling upon him, fluffy gravemound on a living corpse, next day coughing hard; and in a year or two there he sits on the operating table, awake, on a huge galvanized iron platter. They carve his ribs out, like a gardener's sharp clippers pruning suckers, and he can see his own heart beating in the big bell-mirror, if he has the strength, just sitting, like a trussed chicken, sleepier and sleepier, while salt water circulates in his veins, pulsed by a tiny motor-pump. That's how it was.

My poor shy father, first among men and bravest of them all, cheerful beater of time with big white hands, cougher and choral society member, hoarse second tenor who simply stood alongside the other singers in their hats of violet velvet decorated with gold harps, for the half-lung could not stand up to the storms of Beethoven; his body a poplar, his crippled shoulders making him resemble a lightning-struck tree. He did not know what to say when I brought him my first book of verse. I thought he would be happy, proud of me; but he was frightened, trying to conceal his distress. He intended later on to convince my mother that I was led astray by wrong-headedness and obstinacy, since to be a poet was considered on a par with misery and starving to death; and why on earth should I be telling the world all about them, only making trouble for them, for myself, and for the lot of us?

Now that the sullen savage fear of people has melted from my heart, and the bitterness enveloping my being like mist has lifted and I have to shave even twice a day, I understand (and this willed understanding has moulded my soul in its image) that all the members of the bushy-foliaged tree of my relatives are kind, wonderful people, and I should speak about them all, for they are the ingredients, discernible as it were only by chemical analysis, of my childhood, my explosive adolescence, my life, maturing me into a poet. Their character, their healthfulness, most of all their sensibility, have tenderly streaked my heart, like knotty-kneed springy grasses back and forth streaking the earth in the autumn wind. However, I will mention only uncle Jani, my mother's brother, house painter, bass drum in the *schrammel* band, whom perhaps I love best of all. He is always joking, though he has shooting pains in his kidneys, feet and back, and has fallen more than once from his ladder when painting the second floor of apartment buildings. He has had more than a hundred times his share of worries, yet all his words are dew-fresh, sweetly scented like big, full, blood-ringed waxen flowers on August mornings, and his cheerfulness gushes, splashing, like green shoots wet with the sap of gaiety. He too went to work in Budapest by train, like my father. And it was he who brought the news of my father's death. He rang the doorbell that morning; he said not a word. But I could see that grief had cut his yellow face to pieces, his red growth of beard that had sprouted during the mourners' wake had stiffened with agony into a mask. He came inside with a splintered, confused glint in his autumn-blue eyes, shuffling, glanced around, then blurted out like an army order: 'Accept my sincere sympathy.' More was beyond him. He lit a cigarette, and his silence gave me the courage to become an adult for ever after.

My parents' love made me a present of two younger brothers, Gyula born in 1930 and Jancsika in 1932. Jancsika died from meningitis at only ten months. I can remember his birth and his death quite clearly. His birth had jolted Gyula and me into emotions of silence, curiosity, and solemn ceremony, while his death, God only knows why, overwhelmed our hearts with gently dawning joy, standing by his tiny pale blue coffin—the coffin lying on the table, its top leaning against the stove. Jancsika was made of candy, stiffened angel's hair curled about his translucent tiny ears, his folded hands were clouded cellophane gloves, criss-crossed veined blue-stemmed falling insect-wing membraneous leaves, his eyelashes stuck up out of that rosy sleep like spread peacock's tails, while Mama was explaining to us how Jancsika died because he had eaten the label off the bread, which stuck in his tiny penis so that he couldn't pee. Therefore we were not to eat bread labels. That morning was my childhood's Giotto painting: blue enamel sky, gold fan glories amid wild swan-winged, gold-embroidered robed angels—newborn death. Six girls dressed in white carried him to the cemetery on St Michael's pale blue horse, so that he should turn into lily-petals, a crystal death-bell, Child Jesus's gold bell-tinkle, into angels' wings.

My childhood—confusion, round of sorrows, nostalgias, childlike joys, child's pride, unspeakable horrors, fears, and indescribable tangles which memories crowding in do nothing to resolve, I won't even speak of them now. My father was very fond of wine and of friends; my mother liked quiet, order, and books. I often used to cry under the eiderdown, and peacefulness made me very happy. After my fourth year in school my parents entered me in the senior elementary school in Bicske; I used to travel there by train daily from Bia. I spent my whole adolescence travelling, because after that I attended business school in Budapest, although my father would rather I had learned a decent trade. He had tried to get me to enrol as an engineering apprentice in the Gamma Works, where they turned me down, but was keenest of all on my becoming a textile dyer, then regarded as a respectable and well-paid job. I myself was not sure what I really wanted to be. I stayed on in business school, absolutely loathing the profession—bookkeeping, economics, and business arithmetic—but my consuming passion for flying, which developed in secondary school, had already given way to one for poetry, now the centre of my whole existence, with all its afflictions. I spent the summer holidays working on the manor estate as a day-labourer, or with bricklayers as unskilled helper. I spent the evenings reading, flames burning long into the dawn, in the company of poets, mystics, seers, philosophers, my soul in chaos, with wild, crude, and sometimes keenly perceptive intuition. Close to yearning for annihilation, I lived without aim or direction, to my parents' discomfiture, at the kitchen table writing poems or trying to write them, the electric light on till dawn, listening to my father's (awakened by the glare) or to my mother's loving scoldings, or to sterner rebukes, and I rebelled against them. At the slightest pressure I literally exuded decadence, like moisture beading on flower stems when they are squeezed.

Around that time I became the friend, disciple-friend rather, of an art student, Simon Hantai, a budding painter, five years my senior and my mentor, whom I almost worshipped out of love and respect. Although it has been eight years now since I last saw him, I still like to think of him as the embodiment of the arts, with his little paprika-red beard, freckles, vermilion hair, quick impassioned movements, his friendship that was a spur to action, his complete unselfishness; and I feel the same adolescent ardour stirring for him as in the old days, when I had to imitate his way of doing his hair, also his constant inner compulsion to work hard: in short, to keep faith with him. Through the nights he talked to me of Dante, Baudelaire, Babits, of Egyptian and Etruscan Art, about Masaccio and Michelangelo, Picasso and Proust, about modern trends in philosophy, and Cézanne; I would be hard put to list them all here. He gave me their books, showed me their paintings in albums, in periodicals, at home and at the College of Art, and he promised to get my poems published if I wrote some really good ones; he introduced me to his young painter friends, took me along to his college, kept in touch with me by letter, and admitted me to his innermost secrets. We both survived the war in hiding. He, a deserter, and I, just turned sixteen and liable for service in the army, slipped away from Budapest without reporting, fleeing the child-recruit's trepidation, his adolescent male lava-seethings, his ordination for spilling his blood. I went to earth at home up until that Christmas written all over with signal rockets, that empty snakeskin—patterned, cracking—and in the autumn of 1945 we were both living in Budapest again. I was renting a room in Üllői Street; my friend got married and moved into a partly blitzed house on Damjanich Street, the place where I spent most of my evenings, in silence usually, my spirit drooping under blanketing tortuous inferiority, avidly, with a defiant though hidden sense of progressing, and yet in a numbed state, just listening and drifting in a fog, with heart quick to take offence at the slightest thing, happy-unhappy, helplessly, my will falling apart like an unbound sheaf, with my dog's fidelity.

I look back upon those years when I seemed to be staggering in a dazing, choking fog, as if having attained a plateau but still panting hard, becoming more and more drowsy; I seemed paralysed, like one who thinks he is raising arms which in reality hang like a rag-doll's. I was utterly helpless. It was more than I could do to get two lines down on paper together. In fact, I couldn't even express an idea properly. I gave birth to verse, but in a billion mere line-fragments, stillborn from the start; I felt weary in body and spirit. One thing obsessed me: suicide. I never talked about it to anyone, but I was making detailed plans for it, I was incessantly imagining it, preparing myself for it. In the meantime there were born two suitcases-full of verse-ruins and poetic prose influenced by various poets; I saved them up for quite some time, but in the autumn of 1952 I burnt them at home in the garden, along with the potato-stalks. I wrote my university entrance in the summer of 1946. I showed the poems written in those days to some of my teachers, and shortly after, while buying one of Weöres's books at the Zsigmond Móricz bookstore, I met Sándor

Weöres himself. He took quite a liking to my poems, encouraged me, showed me considerable affection, and accepted me as a friend. Then I began to meet other writers as well. I got to know István Kormos during a reading in the university; he invited me to the Café Central and he was the first to get two of my poems published, in the Christmas number of *Diarium* in 1947. My torpor reached its peak between 1946 and 1948, when like someone under a spell, a stranger even to myself, drifting between Bia and Budapest, I lived with my parents. I tried university more than once; I tried to get work too, but I made no money and drifted out of university. I was just hanging around. I was so ashamed. My father was working in a cotton-mill, his half-lung riddled with cavities, his cough getting worse and worse. We were extremely poor: I was wearing father's shirts, suits, and winter coat. I couldn't settle down to work at all. I fell in love with a girl studying to be a chemist, and I smoked my painter-friend's cigarettes. Yes, I was desperately ashamed; and when embarrassment and anxiety brimmed over, and I had had enough of sponging on my parents while I just stagnated like water oozing in the gypsies' pits, teeming with misery's pondweed and bullfrogs, I decided to leave home, and parents who were worrying so much about me, for good. Somewhere I had seen a notice regarding admission to the People's Colleges. I wrote an application, and was admitted to the Attila József College of Literature.

When my parents learned that I had entered university again they welcomed the news, pleased that after all I was going to end up with a university diploma, that they hadn't been providing me with bread and board so long for nothing. For me, residence at the college on Bajza Street meant freedom and survival, even though I was to remain there as a student (pretending to be one, rather) for only about two and a half months, because I had no interest in things academic or in college. Poetry and the literary life were the only things I cared for, especially now that I was living with such young poets as dear, rock-steady László Nagy, that blessed man Gyula Tóth, and the fair-haired, so oddly humble, gentle István Simon. On the second floor, where the women students lived was a wonderful child-girl, her name then Erzsébet Szeverényi; and as I saw her for the first time standing at the top of the staircase on the day I arrived at the college with my modest parcel of belongings, still my timid self, I fell so deeply in love with her that I couldn't help but feel its ache in my bones. We were married shortly after, with two office clerks as witnesses, and having nowhere to go (we were expelled from the college), Erzsike put up with a distant relative for a week, while I moved into Laci Nagy's attic room on Queen Vilma Road, for he was going to be moving over to the Dési-Huber College of Art. The first room we rented together was in Sziv Street. It looked out on that smoke-filled street, and in the early hours of the morning we could hear the drunks, men and women, yelling their heads off, and listen to the clatter of milk carts, the clip-clopping hooves of horses from the Muraköz, horse-shaped large-maned Willendorf Venuses—full-bodied, primeval females, decked out in brass-studded harness, black ribbons, manes plaited with raffia and soft rushes—the shrieking of people getting knifed, of passions running wild. We got it with the help of old Mrs Neumann (the cook at Dési-Huber College, she had a heart of gold); and our first rent-money came from Erzsike's small eider-down, which we took along to a feather-dealer—a Jewish woman with a warty face, deep pores, and feather chin, with fluff in her tousled hair—on Thököly Street, who, after checking our identification against our having stolen it, first offered sixty but actually ended up paying us eighty forints, saying that the moment we entered she could tell she was dealing with someone who was a poet, and if I would only write poems as beautiful as Sándor Petőfi's she was prepared to buy the eiderdown from us without another word.

At this point I shall bring these brief confessions to a close, for they have been leading up to my poetry that was to find expression in book form. Those yearnings to make full confession, beginning with my awareness's primeval chaos, exploding into a star, crumbling into a heavenly body in the thermonuclear reaction of adolescence, in its gravitational catastrophes, the cosmic shaping of the embryo heart growing in the cretaceous period of my existence, filling out full-bodiedly, and yet crested and crowned with bone thorns and bone leaves in my velvet rubbery-skinned flowering, primeval slime-animal dreams—in their giant salamander double-life, their Saurian life, they took wing in my verses' stages of clawed, bone-web winged archaeopteryx, in the hoatzin-cock ancestors; they are throbbing with kettledrums, horns, fiddles, harps, and flutes, and are going on still in that repentance, suffering, agony, qualms of conscience, sorrow which may be ruled only by the tempests of the heart.

[1956, with later revisions]

# Violet-eyed little sister

By my violet-eyed little sister
I sent home, saying I'd be coming,
that I'd do some work on the fences
and put the rose-bushes to bed.
I heard that my mother baked some cakes,
sieving flour for them from
the bottom of the sack, the drawer's corners,
and dusted off her floury apron.
She laid the table with a clean cloth,
warm goat's milk was in the mug,
my white shirt, spread out freshly ironed
shone waiting for me on the bed.
My father sliced tobacco leaves
for me to blow smoke-rings; he'd gathered up
a basketful of dry stalks and shavings
and lit a fire, so I wouldn't shiver:
white paper won't keep out the cold.
From early morning they stood at the gate,

shuffling their feet, coughing now and then,
looking up at the sky, then down the street,
they smiled at the boy herding the cattle,
they'd picked a bouquet of numb Michaelmas daisies.
As I didn't come, they stood there felled
by frost, only their sighs rustling;
the autumn wind was breaking loose
scattering thick rime down on their heads.

[1949]

# The foaling time

With May roses on the bush breaking
and elderbush in bloom, and lilacs—
the mare would know it was her time to foal:
she'd rest more often, and hobble in her walk.

A little boy paced her gently around,
walking the flowering fields to a song;
by the time they turned homeward tired,
the moon on a hump of blue sky swung.

In her stable-pen, on soft straw,
moist with foam, she would tremble now;
while heaving heavily, watching on,
reclined the swollen-bellied cows.

And so, when even hay-ricks dozed,
and the Seven Stars aimed south—
she foaled her young. Then long she licked
him on the wet-shut eyes and mouth.

The newcomer slumbered at his mother's side,
lay like plucked down of pillow-stuff;
straw was never spread so fine,
nor sleeping snow, nor milk, so soft.

In a red cap the bright dawn came up,
gave a hello and went for a sprint.
The colt got up on lean knobby legs
and tottered, like water wavering.

And as the morning stuck its blue nose
in at the window, sniffing them both,
the young one nudged at his mother's side
and sought the milk with wet-soft mouth.

The leaves made stir by fits and starts,
and cheerful chickens scraped for chaff,
while up above, for envy wilting,
the golden petalled stars dropped off.

[1949]

*L. D.*

# Song of the tractor

Kneel down, all you meek little horses,
today the co-operative got a new tractor,
a green-painted, thirty-horsepower
rubber-wheeled motor-tractor.

On Sunday the men still hung around it,
with smiling eyes admiring it.
They stroked it, tried out its iron saddle,
and fooled with the steering wheel.

Monday it was ploughing merrily.
It pulled four ploughs all at once;
it exhaled water from its shining nose
and back-fired smoke-rings.

Kneel down, all you meek little horses,
all you foals with a star on your forehead.
This tractor is a colt of fire and iron.
Petrol he feeds on, and oil.

Look, we are ploughing the downy earth;
above us a skylark sings;
clouds race in the blue wind,
and our hearts sing for happiness.

Now it is noon: we are resting, the tractor and I.
A blue flower bends down to my forehead.
A spotted heifer comes from the meadow—
she smells me, and stops beside me.

[1950]

*A. J. M. S.*

# Farm,
# at dark,
# on the
# Great Plain

Tingling,
sparkling,
smouldering,
over the mute earth the loosed night falls.

Glass-petalled flowers, leaves of thin glass
are incandescent, as
our anguish.

Peculiar weeds, lush and fine-spun
dream on,
half in the dark secreted
their torsos reaching up into the void
like the brooding undergrowth at the bottom of the soul.
Suffering and sin flare up in every blade.

The parts are not the whole.
In the lucid earth-dark all is corruptible.

Agleam is all
that juts up out of the gloaming:
roofslant, poplar,
lip of the trough,
moon-tilted swallow soaring, homing
flittering,
the hay-rick's ripe-gold keening.
Among the stubble pheasants move and rustle,
the young deer nibble.
They shy away from the hare's wide-open eyes
and veer out of the light.

The moonlight's liquid glass
wells over the earth
and quells the very silence in its clasp
to crystal blocks,
glass turrets,
tinkling vine-stems.
Still—how this silence (silvery bushes,
half-guessed-at-stalks, dim files of foliage)
entangles and engulfs the din of empty space
and murmurous flower-scent from the garden-beds.

The house squats
hunched like a scarab, lest
the Milky Way reach down its scaly talons.

The sap in the bean-vines slowly
pulses and throbs

and the withery pods down in the dark recover
a new-born firmness. They discover life only
in building it, never knowing their lot.
Minerals, crystals, water,
the flesh-filling cucumber
drinks in, swelling its small rhinoceros-hide.

While sap (like mother's-blood to a darkling
embryo) seeps through the cells,
whole solar systems circle
within, galaxies countless, crackling
as they plummet and weave:
so, breathless, matter lives.

All things are incandescent with their light of being:
the moon . . . the moon dwells on its waning;
the breathing tree on how its leaves must fall;
the melon feels its juices sweetening up;
autumn's vinegar-steam the tomatoes ponder;
the corn senses its kernels' thrust from the cob —
they have started already to form
like pearls in an infant's gum —
standing mindless and mild the horses sleep
or dream of trailing down again for water
and the whinnying gallop after.

The sow breathes heavily, deep in her slumber.
Against her belly piglets scramble
and swarm
like a moving pulp of warm
craving, a rosy greediness.
The cabbage-stalks harden and ridge.

Under uprights and open thatch
lie cartwheels, boards, scrap-iron, trash.
The spiderwebs' gauze-cities swing and dangle.
On the warm dungheap the ducks snuggle,
and its breath flutters the nettle's candlewick
and nearby wheat and rosemary-spikes flicker.

Stubble, corn, hempfields stretch out all around
far off, where darkness is intense as sound.
The moon shepherds the flocks.
And to the listening field-mouse an assured bull-frog croaks.

I lie in the drenched grass.
Spice-perfumes and my senses here converse.
These flower-cups are metal-froth let cool.
The ground-flow of air stirs
and wafts warmth to me from the stubble-fields,
and honey-smell—
commingled
yet distinct fragrances.
Strange, blissful night, primal, voluptuous—
random—with nothing of passion's single-mindedness.
Plant cannot guess—nor planet—the knowledge a human bears.

Even a man knows little, has but dimly understood
how marble is one substance with milk of dandelion
and prismed insects' eyes
and blood.
Yet, as a man I am removed,
set apart from dews
or Pleiades.
In me alone is the tumult of human cares, and of love—
my pain, my power, are from these.

From the old earth-soaked dark—silence's floor
writhing with stems and storm of sap—to the clear
lift of the upper silences, one free, unbridled power
of teeming: the exploding star
fusing in a primeval shower
of metal-mist, condensed, compounded. Ore
vomited to the crucible where
blast-furnace slag floods off, the slower
seminal globules, crystallizing, or
vegetation's jelly and mulch, its queer
seeds, like the winking elements in the core
of the fissured rock, all crushed in pluvial fire,
molten to become matter, all afire
to become real, till the quarries
of chlorophylled purpose mire
and melt in a plastic flow
and the foam of glossy light
crams to anthracite.
With ululating, jungle-roar,
tremors of flaring fear,
in mawling, ravening desire,
rivered with sweat ... the everlasting flood
seethes and simmers on, in solitude.

I love you. You can be aware of it—
after all, something new,
different from the love helpless matter feels,
with its heedlessness of tomorrow.
No falling star can hear when my heart calls.
The man is sleeping in his corner, the hiss
of his breath catching at a rheumatic crick.
In the kitchen the flickering oil-lamp plays

over the woman as she leans
dozing against the wall.
Her old knuckles and veins
under the lamplight show a yellow glaze.
They are both making ready to die,
for this too must be done.

The splayed furniture strains for a voice remote past time.
Sap rises in its dreams.
Leaves sigh, ring wells on ring within.
Whining in sleep, it is washed once more by a forest moon.

A foot-clout by the bed,
beside one lumpy boot.
On the wall a picture from an old paper
pinned flat.
A derelict watch-chain on another hook.
A book mourning, unread.

By now I know for sure what I half-glimpsed before:
how senseless your life would be, all by yourself, alone,
and how it would be for me too, a desolate rolling-stone—
sadness and brute desire.
For animals do not need
to be one till they rot.
They feed, suckle their young, kill, make water, mate,
physical to the hilt.
And when star melts into star, and all the heavens move
the foaming metals flash, and spin, and fade,
the molten passions lapse, dissolve,
all by themselves.
Mollusc and vermin couple just to breed.

Only with you I believe, I feel at one,
nor need my heart at last go so mercilessly alone
to its corruption.

Flower and plant filaments slowly to new
forms glimmer.
The earth bears fruit in an unwitting flow.
Thatch, poplar, cornstalks shimmer.
And I look on as it topples almost in my face,
scaly-bellied, soft, and huge-as-earth,
hiding its reptile head among ancient galaxies,
its tail dangling over in some other night of space,
the jewelled, gelatinous Milky Way, its girth
brushing against the lamenting corn-silk
and the world's bulk.

[1954]

*M. A.*

# Black
# peacock

Angles, straight lines, points, indentations,
in this head balance. Burnished, veined, its block holds them.
Sad bottom eyelids lie within
washtub rims of galvanized iron.

    Pista, remember the snowy night moaning:
    'Jesus, too, had his green tree to shoulder!'
    'Kormos Pista's girl lies with another'.

Slumped over, old tombstone, brooding,
women's shoulders jostling him.
What tears he has are pearl-handled knives,
his words are incandescent vibrations.

    Pista, old friend, do you remember it?
    We sat on the Danube's marble parapet,
    we were aching for love, and we wept.

He has no father and no mother.
Perhaps God invented him, in order
to absolve Himself from sin.
Where he, the Phoenix, brushes dust, white flowers gleam.

Remember, do you remember, Pista,
that winter sky, white with news of neon,
we wept: can one love again, again live on?

Across his heart struts a black peacock, singing.
Try to speak: he leans away, brooding, not answering.
He says nothing:  the proud peacock's step he's watching.
He only weeps: the peacock's song possessing him.

Pista, remember, as friends we were near,
when love lay in a bottle of beer,
love just two rails in the moonlight here.

Do not divide him up amongst you, women,
like famished prisoners some sweet bun.
Sorrows, stop tearing at him,
like hawk-women over the love of a dying man.

Pista, remember, just the other day,
I'd end it all, you heard me say,
if what I have a right to were denied me.

All you who know how to love, kill for love,
put off hating him, there will be time enough
when of angles, indentations, straight lines, points,
nothing but balancing lame silence remains.

[1955]

# At
# twenty-six

Twenty-six years are few enough to force me, terrified,
to shriek aloud: 'Frost is tinfoil in my skull of bone!'
Yet was I given to loving, cursing, burying whatever had died
    —and not for myself alone.

Fate, destiny or something will yet give me time
—and enough strength also to my faith—
that what pains only myself I may cry aloud in a rhyme
    before my death.

My flowers are still wet with dew. By sickness my life's not corroded.
In my fields strut peacocks, bulls stand, foam-lathered colts start.
I stand firm. Flaming galaxies are exploded
    by a kiss—in my heart.

Soon maybe my flowers will shrivel to straw. Hailstone,
brimstone, will shatter my green shoots, my green place.
But, ah, till then let me flame and thunder on
    —a golden stallion of Space.

How soon? Who knows? What do I care?
I am alive—an exploding resplendent world.
And if I collide with another star
    out of its orbit it's hurled.

Who else could make men believe
what only I know
and which if the heart but dimly conceive,
    horror-struck, it begins to glow?

Do not fear for me. I am resolute and immutable.
If this be a virtue, it is mine then.
Upsurges from my lips the ineffable
    quality of man.

                    [1954]

*A. J. M. S.*

# Crown
# of hatred
# and love

Oh how I hated that village, crown of thorns around my timid child's heart, at whose whimpering response to some pulsation, some birdcall from the constellations, it would bite with round tangled mouth, cruel teeth-circle, so that my larva-soft flesh bled from within towards the surface, towards the stars, and on my starwards-yearning flesh the skin flowered with freckles, like the blue graveyard dotted with All Souls' Eve candles, so that I felt my heart pouring through my limbs, bleeding like Gulyás Pál's massive-headed, mosquito larva's translucent Christ-like staggering body, about whom once I wanted to write perhaps one of my epics' most important lines.

Oh how I hated that village, closing around me like a spined mollusc, each thorn's tip a tenacious leech's mouth, a belly beneath the hard grey shield around its malevolent hideousness like a war-horse's iron head-armour, from whose embossed orifice only the hairy muzzle's flower-whorl protrudes with whetted teeth behind spongy fur-skinned mouth's petals to sink into me, chew up my warm entrails, sip them, suck them in: this wreath of thorn-mouths woven of a thousand visored horses' heads! This living star-crown seeking refuge in stone cisterns, only its outer casing deflects the teeth, while beneath all is crumbling decay, wasting savage hungers!

Oh how I hated that village, black blinkers for my longing, absurd, clever, shining colt's wide eyes. They fastened them round my forehead to keep me from seeing as far as Sirius, that my wondering eyes should not— beyond the drifting iceflow of light-years—find answering radiance in the spring-scented fields of light from other worlds!

Oh how I hated those black blinkers, my vision's stables, set deep in my frontal bones and which I could rub aside from my eyes only by butting at the far-off star-cliffs screaming out at the terrifying kisses of ores!

Oh how I hated that village, those merciless scissors screeching open rusty hands to clip sprouting wing-feathers—slimy-sticky still like a shell-hatched chick's, like the yellow wolf's-milk that oozes in the weeds on the hillside graveyard. I hated that stony egg, straining to crack its obstinate shield, beneath which Darkness and Light were living together as in the universe; and I kept turning and turning about in the glistening embryo-fluids, with clinging pond-weedy eyelashes, nostrils stopped with viscid blood, with tongue driven back down my throat, with lungs sagging in the starved air like cellophane-straining wrapped rosebushes, so dilated by now as to fill the entire egg, faltering in its choking grip like a failing heart, for I had swollen into the pitted shell's texture, my body shrivelling, my being driven within itself by solitude's slippery concavity.

O my Village, you swamp-toad, holding fast upon the Titan-skulls of putrescent ancestors in the universe's translucent deeps, glass throat of silence, gently rhythmical cell-basket, ravenous cobweb funnel, wide-mouthed sack of pulsing fibre-animals, you submarine white spectral belly, monster mildness in the marbling bell-strokes of the moon, who subdues in its passage through you the onrushing universe, its terrific flames, feathery-crested prodigious life-mass, shy crab-droplet tears, crystalline animal-bloods.

O my Village, you flower-fragrant calf's moist cherry-muzzle thirsting

for the udders of world-mists netted with rubies, why did I hate you? My
morning's gold-fenced flower garden, why did I dread you? Why did I not
weep for you, my childhood?

2

Frost covers the rose-trees; a few scraggy geese stand
with lead-laced wings trailing forlornly on the ground.
Octopus arms of plants wetly catch at bullfrogs.
Like dried-up jellyfish a few torn snowy rags;
long potato-stalks straggle out, limp and brown
like chicken's entrails that dried where they were thrown;
parsley alone stands out green, that frost stiffens
in porcelain feathers of colour and silence.

The brown towers of burrs from hawthorn and thistle
are like tatters of mourning in a burned-out chapel,
like an empty wasps' nest's smoked-out architecture.
Thistles and saplings jut out from the plastered wall,
and propped there, stick-limbs knotted, helm of mossy metal,
skeleton-membrane shirted, a locust's empty shell,
image of knight's armour in dusty mother-of-pearl.

One tree still stands leaning, lightning-stallion torn,
dreaming on, while a crow caws from its glass crown.
Down from the picket-fence some rusted wreath-wires hang,
and a broken bucket lies musing on a plank.
The lilacs are creatures guided by other stars.
Hollow-toothed white hen-coops stagger with doors ajar,
just one hen left scratching about in blue manure,
picking at the bones of the cock who had her.

Proud I was, too stupid to be good, a thickhead,
not once did I listen to what my father said,
I left this house behind, with no goodbyes from me.
Slowly, humility put out leaves within me!
My heart, with birds' whirrings once inoculated,
yearned to fly away, into infinity melted,
spending itself in shame, and untrue to its nest.
Now I can only weep, here in my grief wordless.

Where is he who stayed here, and would not renounce me?
In his hot coffin he's fermenting, mould-furry!
He who poured out new wine lazily, who suffered
on his pearl-crusted face my prickly bobbing head,
scolding me so I'd weep, gazing at the smoke-palms,
to whom I would recite 'The Death of György Dózsa'?
The carrion-larvaed star has drunk him up, while I
was lulled in the god's lap who always was to lie.

Where's my father now? Where? Where's my pride of those days?
I became a rainbow, and he maggoty clay.

[1963]

# The boy
# changed into
# a stag cries
# out at the
# gate of secrets

Her own son the mother called
from afar crying,
her own son the mother called
from afar crying,
she went before the house from there calling,
her hair's full knot she loosed,
with it the dusk wove a dense quivering
veil, a precious cloak down to her ankles,
wove a stiff mantle, heavy-flaring,
a flag for the wind with ten black tassels
a shroud, the fire-stabbed blood-tainted dusk.
Her fingers she twined in the sharp tendrilled

stars, her face the moon's foam coated,
and on her own son she called shrilly
as once she called him, a small child,
she went before the house and talked to the wind,
with songbirds spoke, sending swiftly
words after the wild pairing geese,
to the shivering bullrushes,
to the potato-flower so silvery,
to the clench-balled bulls rooted so firmly,
to the well-shading fragrant sumach tree,
she spoke to the fish leaping at play,
to the mauve oil-rings afloat fleetingly:
 you birds and boughs, hear me
listen as I cry out,
 and listen, you fishes, you flowers
listen, for I speak to be heard,
 listen you glands of expanding soils
  you vibrant fins, astral-seeding parachutes,
 decelerate, you humming motors of the saps
 in the depths of the atom, screw down the whining taps,
  all metal-pelvised virgins, sheep alive under cotton
listen as I cry out,
for I'm crying out to my son!

 Her own son the mother called
her cry ascending in a spiral,
 within the gyre of the universe it rose,
her limbs flashing in the light rays
like the back of a fish slippery-scaled
or a roadside boil of salt or crystal.
 Her own son the mother called:
come back, my own son, come back

    I call you, your own mother!
come back, my own son, come back
    I call you, your mild harbour,
come back, my own son, come back
    I call you, your cool fountain,
come back, my own son, come back
    I call you, your memory's teat,
come back, my own son, come back
    I call you, your withered tent,
come back, my own son, come back
    I call you, your almost sightless lamp.


Come back, my own son, for I'm blind in this world of sharp
                               objects,
within yellow-green bruises my eyes are sinking, my brow contracts,
my thighs—my barked shins,
from all sides things rush at me like crazed wethers,
the gate, the post, the chair try their horns on me
doors slam upon me like drunken brawlers,
the perverse electricity shoots its current at me,
my flaking skin seeps blood—a bird's beak cracked with a stone,
    scissors swim out of reach like spider crabs all metal,
the matches are sparrows' feet, the pail swings back at me with its
                            handle,
come back, my own son, come back
my legs no longer carry me like the young hind,
    vivid tumours pout on my feet
    gnarled tubers penetrate my purpling thighs,
on my toes grow bony structures,
    the fingers on my hands stiffen, already the flesh is shelly
scaling like slate from weathered geologic formations,
    every limb has served its time and sickens,

come back, my own son, come back,
    for I am no more as I was,
    I am gaunt with inner visions
    which flare from the stiffening hoary organs
    as on winter mornings an old cock's crowing
rings from a fence of shirts, hanging hard-frozen,
I call you, your own mother,
come back, my own son, come back,
to the unmanageable things bring a new order,
discipline the estranged objects, tame the knife,
    domesticate the comb,
for I am now but two gritty green eyes
glassy and weightless like the *libellula*
whose winged nape and dragon jaws, you know it well
    my son, hold so delicately
two crystal apples in his green-lit skull,
I am two staring eyes without a face
seeing all, now one with unearthly beings.
Come back, my own son, come back,
    with your fresh breath, set all to rights again.

      In the far forest the lad heard,
      at once he jerked up his head,
      with his wide nostrils testing
      the air, soft dewlaps pulsing
      with veined ears pricked, harkening
      alertly to those tones sobbing
      as to a hunter's slimy tread,
      or hot wisps curling from the bed
      of young forest fires, when smoky
      high woods start to whimper bluely.
      He turned his head, no need to tell

him this was the voice he knew so well,
now by an agony he's seized,
fleece on his buttocks he perceives,
in his lean legs sees the proof
of strange marks left by each cleft hoof,
where lilies shine in forest pools
sees his low hairy-pursed buck-balls.
He pushes his way down to the lake
breasting the brittle willow brake,
rump slicked with foam, at each bound
he slops white froth on the hot ground,
his four black hooves tear out a path
through wild flowers wounded to death,
stamp a lizard into the mould
neck swollen, tail snapped, growing cold.
And when he reached the lake at last
into its moonlit surface glanced:
it holds the moon, beeches shaking,
and back at him a stag staring!
Only now thick hair does he see
covering all his slender body
hair over knees, thighs, the transverse
tasselled lips of his male purse,
his long skull had sprouted antlers
into bone leaves their bone boughs burst,
his face is furry to the chin
his nostrils are slit and slant in.
Against trees his great antlers knock,
veins knot in ropes along his neck,
madly he strains, prancing he tries
vainly to raise an answering cry,
only a stag's voice bells within

the new throat of this mother's son,
he drops a son's tears, paws the brink
to banish that lake-monster, sink
it down into the vortex sucking
fluid dark, where scintillating
little fish flash their flowery fins,
minute, bubble-eyed diamonds.
The ripples subside at last in the gloom,
but a stag still stands in the foam of that moon.

Now in his turn the boy cries back
   stretching up his belling neck,
now in his turn the boy calls back
   through his stag's throat, through the fog calling:
   mother, my mother
   I cannot go back,
   mother, my mother
   you must not lure me,
   mother, my mother
   my dear breeding nurse,
   mother, my mother
   sweet frothy fountain,
   safe arms that held me
   whose heavy breasts fed me
   my tent, shelter from frosts,
   mother, my mother
   seek not my coming,
   mother, my mother
   my frail silken stalk,
   mother, my mother
   bird with teeth of gold,
   mother, my mother,
   you must not lure me!

If I should come home
my horns would fell you,
from horn to sharp horn
I'd toss your body,
if I should come home
down I would roll you,
tread your loose veiny
breasts mangled by hooves,
I'd stab with unsheathed
horns, maul with my teeth,
tread in your womb even.
If I should come home
mother, my mother
I'd spill out your lungs
for blue flies buzzing round,
and the stars would stare down
into your flower-organs
which once did hold me,
with warmth of summer suns,
in shiny peace encased
where warmth never ceased,
as once cattle breathed
gently to warm Jesus.
Mother, my mother
do not summon me,
death would strike you down
in my shape's coming
if this son drew near.
Each branch of my antlers
is a gold filament,
each prong of my antlers
a winged candlestick,

each tine of my antlers
a catafalque candle,
each leaf of my antlers
a gold-laced altar.
Dead surely you'd fall
if you saw my grey antlers
soar into the sky
like the All Soul's Eve
candle-lit graveyard,
my head a stone tree
leafed with growing flame.
Mother, my mother
if I came near you
I would soon singe you
like straw, I would scorch
you to greasy black clay,
you'd flare like a torch
for I would roast you
to charred shreds of flesh.
Mother, my mother
do not summon me
for if I came home
I would devour you,
for if I came home
your bed I would ravage,
the flower garden
with my thousand-pronged
horns would I savage,
I'd chew through the trees
in the stag-torn groves,
drink dry the one well
in a single gulp,

if I should return
I'd fire your cottage,
and then I would run
to the old graveyard,
with my pointed soft
nose, with all four hooves
I'd root up my father,
with my teeth wrench off
his cracked coffin lid
and snuff his bones over!
Mother, my mother
do not lure me,
I cannot go back,
for if I came home
I'd bring your death surely.

In a stag's voice the lad cried,
and in these words his mother answered him:
 come back, my own son, come back
I call you, your mother.
 Come back my own son, come back
I'll cook you brown broth, and you'll slice onion-rings in it,
they'll crunch between your teeth like quartz splinters in a giant's jaws,
I'll give you warm milk in a clean jug,
from my last keg trickle wine into heron-necked bottles,
and I know how to knead the bread with my rocky fists, I know how
              you like it,
bread to bake soft-bellied buns for you, sweet bread for the feasts,
 come back, my own son, come back
from the live breasts of the screeching geese for your eiderdown
            I plucked feathers,

weeping I plucked my weeping geese, the spots stripped of
feathers turning
a fierce white on their breasts, like the mouths of the dying,
I shook up your pallet in the clear sunlight, made it fresh for your rest,
the yard has been swept, the table is laid—for your coming.


O mother, my mother
for me there's no homecoming,
do not lay out for me twisted white bread
or sweet goat's milk in my flowered mug foaming,
and do not prepare for me a soft bed,
for feathers ravage not the breasts of the geese,
spill your wine rather, upon my father's grave let it soak in,
the sweet onions bind into a garland,
fry up for the little ones that froth-bellying dough.
The warm milk would turn to vinegar at my tongue's lapping,
into a stone turtle you'd see the white bread changing,
your wine within my tumbler like red blood rising,
the eiderdown would dissolve into little blue flames in silence
and the brittle-beaked mug splinter into swordgrass.
O mother, O mother, my own good mother
my step may not sound in the paternal house,
I must live deep in the green wood's underbrush
no room for my tangled antlers in your shadowy
house, no room in your yard for my cemetery
antlers; for my foliated horns are a loud world-tree
their leaves displaced by stars, their green moss by the Milky Way,
sweet-scented herbs must I take in my mouth, only
the first-growth grasses can my spittle liquefy,
I may no longer drink from the flowered mug you bring
only from a clean spring, only from a clean spring!

I do not understand, do not understand your strange tortured words, my son
you speak like a stag, a stag's soul seems to possess you, my unfortunate one.
When the turtle-dove cries, the turtle-dove cries, when the little
                bird sings, the little bird sings, my son
wherefore am I—in the whole universe am I the last lost
                soul left, the only one?
Do you remember, do you remember your small once-young
                mother, my son?
I do not understand, do not understand your sad tortured words,
                my long-lost son.

Do you remember how you came running, running home to me
                so happy with your school report,
    you dissected a bull-frog, spreading out on the fence his
                freckled webbed paddle-feet,
and how you pored over the books on aircraft, how you followed
                me in to help with the washing,
    you loved Irene B., your friends were V. J.
    and H. S. the wild orchid-bearded painter,
and do you remember on Saturday nights, when your father came
                home sober, how happy you were?

O mother, my mother, do not speak of my sweetheart of old
                nor of my friend,
    like fish they fleet by in cold depths, the vermilion-chinned painter
    who knows now where he has gone his shouting way, who
                knows mother, where my youth has gone?
Mother, my mother, do not recall my father, out of his flesh
                sorrow has sprouted,
    sorrow blossoms from the dark earth, do not recall
                my father, my father,
    from the grave he'd rise, gathering about him his yellowed bones,
    from the grave stagger, hair and nails growing anew.

Oh, Oh, Uncle Wilhelm came, the coffin-maker, that puppet-faced man,
    he told us to take your feet and drop you neatly in the coffin,
    I retched because I was afraid, I had come straight home
                from Pest that day;
    you also, my father, went back and forth to Pest, you were
                only an office messenger, the rails twisted up,
    oh, the stabbing knives in my belly then, shadows from the
                candle ravined your tight cheeks.
Your new son-in-law, Laci the barber, shaved you that day, the
                candle dribbling the while like a silent baby
    regurgitating its glistening entrails, its long luminous nerves like vines,
    the choral society stood round you in their purple hats
                mourning you at the tops of their voices,
    with one finger I traced the rim of your forehead,
                your hair was alive still,
    I heard it grow, I saw the bristles sprout from your chin
    blackened by morning; the next day your throat had sunk
                beneath snake-grass stalks of hair,
    its curve like a soft-furred cantaloup, the colour of a yellow-haired
                caterpillar upon blue cabbage skin.
Oh, and I thought your hair, your beard, would overgrow
                the whole room, the yard,
    the entire world, stars nestling like cells in its hiving strands.
Ah! heavy green rain started then to fall, the team of red
                horses before the hearse neighed in terror,
    one lashing out above your head with a lightning bolt hoof,
                the other relentlessly pissing
    so that his purple parts passed out with it like a hanged
                man's tongue, while their coachman cursed
    and the downpour washed round the huddled brassbandsmen,
                then all those old friends blew with a will,
    sobbing as they played, beside the globe-thistle studded chapel wall,

those old friends blew till their lips swelled blue, and the tune
                    spiralled out and up,
the old friends blew with cracked lips bleeding now,
                    with eyeballs staring,
blew for the card games and booze, the bloated, the withered
                    and the trumped women,
played you out for the red-letter day beer-money, the tips
                    sent whirling into space after you
they blew, sobbing as they blew sadly down into the
                    sedimentary layers of silted sadness,
music pouring from the burnished mouths, from rings of brass
                    into putrescent nothingness,
out of it streamed the petrified sweethearts, rotting women,
                    and mouldy grandfathers in the melody,
with small cottages, cradles, and rolling like onions a generation
                    of enamel-swollen, silver-bodied watches,
Easter bells and multifarious saviours came out also on
                    wide-spreading wings of sound
that summoned up satchels, railway wheels, and soldiers
                    brass-buttoned at the salute,
the old friends played on, teeth reddening behind lips curled
                    back and swollen like blackened liver,
and yourself conducting the choir—Well done, boys, that's
                    grand, carry it on, don't stop now!—
all the time with hands clasped tight, those gold spiders with
                    huge spoke-joint knotted legs, resting on
                    your heart,
in the cupboard your collapsed boots await the relations, white
                    socks naked on your bread-crust curling feet,
old friends that day played you out in the crashing rain,
                    valves snapping like steel Adam's apples
like fangs of antediluvian birds, teeth of the *carcharodon* looking
                    for carrion from out those brass trumpets.

O mother, my mother, do not recall my father,
    let my father be, lest his eyes burst out of the reopening earth.


   Her own son the mother called
       from afar crying:
come back, my own son, come back
       turn away from that stone world,
you stag of the stone woods, industrialized air, electric grids,
chemical lightnings, iron bridges, and streetcars lap up your blood,
day by day they make a hundred assaults on you,
                yet you never hit back,
it is I calling you, your own mother,
       come back, my own son, come back.


   There he stood on the renewing crags of time,
stood on the ringed summit of the sublime
universe, there stood the boy at the gate of secrets,
his antler prongs were playing with the stars,
with a stag's voice down the world's lost paths
he called back to his life-giving mother:
       mother, my mother, I cannot go back,
pure gold seethes in my hundred wounds,
day by day a hundred bullets knock me from my feet
and day by day I rise again, a hundred times more complete,
day by day I die three billion times,
day by day I am born three billion times,
each branch of my antlers is a dual-based pylon,
each prong of my antlers a high-tension wire,
my eyes are ports for ocean-going merchantmen, my veins
              are tarry cables, these
teeth are iron bridges, and in my heart surge the
           monster-infested seas,

5*

each vertebra is a teeming metropolis, for a spleen I have a
                    smoke-puffing barge,
each of my cells is a factory, my atoms are solar systems,
sun and moon swing in my testicles, the Milky Way is
                    my bone marrow,
each point in space is one part of my body,
my brain's impulse is out in the curling galaxies.

Lost son of mine, come back for all that,
your *libellula*-eyed mother watches for you still.

Only to die will I return, only to die come back,
yes, I will come, will come to die,
and when I have come—but to die—my mother,
then may you lay me in the parental house,
with your marbled hands you may wash my body,
my glandulous eyelids close with a kiss.
    And then, when my flesh falls apart
and lies in its own stench, yet deep in flowers,
    then shall I feed on your blood, be your body's fruit,
then shall I be your own small son again,
and this shall give pain to you alone, mother,
    to you alone, O my mother.

[1955]

# Sorrow bred
# to perfection

Potato-bloom, potato-bloom,
fair sorrow, bred to perfection.

Numbness of my mother's garden,
potato-bloom, potato-bloom.

Behind parsley, dill, and verdant
poppy's slumber, potato-plant,

potato-bloom, potato-bloom,
mild sorrow, bred to perfection.

Paris, New York, I'd view their towers
but see instead your cell-born towers.

I'd watch the sea's fish sparkling
but see only your bloom foaming,

potato-bloom, potato-bloom,
gentle cousin, potato-bloom.

Below, where the purpling clay drains
into darkness, the bulging brains;

above shakes your flowered gloom,
potato-bloom, potato-bloom,

a faint wick-light guttering out,
green catafalque, potato-plant,

green love, making lilac-yellow
flesh-quivers for his love-arrow,

speaking to the envoys of space,
visiting ultra-violet rays.

Potato-bloom, potato-bloom,
you sorrow, bred to perfection,

you're no different from what I am,
the deathly hope of every man,

on this sea-bed's dried-out, well-kept
cultivated plot, wheel of light,

knot of women, all on one stem,
potato-plant, potato-bloom.

The same fluid that in you wells
up through your length, between your cells,

stirs the blissful animals, and
the inhuman grief of humans.

Exploding seeds, deep in soft flesh
bringing light, ascend with a rush,

and broodingly set floating free,
senses rebelling beautifully,

with the blood's hydraulic pressure
your being's glass-fragile structure.

Your deft mirrors, light-gathering,
understand hydrogen's exploding,

and transmit its detonation,
using the sun's self-destruction.

Ferny kisses, phase of quiet,
potato-bloom, potato-plant.

You too were the dream of the sea,
flower of my fidelity,

in you wheels up the perfect rose,
swaying, choked, stripped before it goes

hugging you, its one-eyed sister,
unconscious and impassive star.

I'd view London's iron bridges
but see instead your petals' arches.

You're no different from what I am,
the deathly hope of every man,

man's dreamed substantiality,
flower of my fidelity,

you sorrow, bred to perfection,
potato-bloom, potato-bloom.

[1955]

# Seasons

Sped is Autumn! And decay is sped.
  I tore towards you across the rotting plants.
My helpless eyes hid behind the vacant lids of the dead,
like solitary naked crabs in pearl-rimmed shells.
Dead men's shadows run purple from the whale-tooth railings.
Mouldering babies hang from their maw, and moaning
                         soiled chrysanthemums.
A blue dove they led towards me, her feet belled silver
                         chains trailing.
I slumped before your atom-splitting smile, turned grey
                    under your wandering glance.

  And Winter's gone! Unlike others we knew.
  The city's jaw of bells gnaws the bald heavens.
My teeth machine-gun the cold streets, where I begged bread for you.
Winter ties up the woods in silence, knotting the white ends.
Hyacinth-blue the shadows from fairyland, behind that railing,
up to your silent window lope animals in a sorrowing throng.
Grey ruin hugging the lilac, at your bedside I listen to
                  your heedless babbling,
deer, hare, and thrush in the marked snow follow your flame-white song.

Pitiless Spring! Foam encrusts the walls,
   organic green flesh has dried in a cracked glaze,
  shreds of dead flowers shrivel beside spooled tendrils,
   death's whirling arms for the bright seed grains reach from outer space.
  Shadows vomit up green bile beside the railing,
cannibal sharks and saw-tooth starfish thrash hungry in swarms,
lust sprouts at your dribbled prayers, chuckles, and happy gabbling.
I throw myself here, grass on living grave, covering breasts
                              fragrant as tombs.


And in time Summer! Into a gold medal it mints a people.
   The moon's randy stallion flashes his badge with a blue grin,
  beneath ropes of nerves, cries of pain rise from the world.
  In ultra-violet froth the insect slavers in its daydream.
Acid shadows are licking from the snake-fang railing,
lizard fingers grasp at your bulging heart, where many moths
                              to red ash burned.
Under the hardening leaves, I listen to your female flower's
                              husky moaning,
groaning by the red cave's dripstone garden, great panther, I,
                              in your heart buried.

                                        [1957]

# Four voices: non-maledictory, in lament and supplication

Stars turn, gold nipples hissing,
   a hare's shed coat drifts in air, a scarecrow thistle weeps tears of frost,
oh what can you, little one, what can you know of death, my love,
         what can you know of it, for heaven's sake!
Stars revolve, eyeballs roll in numb sockets screeching,
among silver altars and silver bracken deranged eyeballs searching,
with herds of gold bison sobbing, with drunken stallion-gods whinnying,
stars boil revolving, from un-being live steam scalds away cold's ache,
oh what can you, little one, what can you know of death, my love,
         what can you know of it, for heaven's sake!
Whitened, dried up, from the knot-jointed knuckle-fringed grasses
       hangs hoarfrost,
beards at the mallows' breasts, reed-stubble's shaggy nape grey with frost,
   white death in thistledown, in rotting potato stalk,

in white mould on bullrushes alighting swanlike,
oh what can you, little one, what can you know of death, my love,
      what can you know of it, for heaven's sake!
A gold chain twistingly weaves around and around
  the silver unicorn's breast, forehead,
his blue nostrils snort stiff-rimmed with black blood,
oh what can you, little one, what can you know of death, my love,
      what can you know of it, for heaven's sake!
The earth, earth through its flesh noiselessly seeps blood
  drying upon fresh-dug twilight loam,
oh what can you, little one, what can you know of death, my love,
      what can you know of it, for heaven's sake!
Nothingness quakes, a hairless tiny animal,
it cannot cry out, whimper, nor squeal,
  festering teethmarks in its blueing skin
are the stars with septic light, swollen rim,
only we, the more mortal parts of nothingness, know how to mourn,
whom existence roughly thrusts
outside like day-old sightless pups
  set out in the bone-chill by a hard farmer,
nuzzling feebly, crawling, reaching for hot belly, rosy teat,
oh what can you, little one, what can you know of death, my love,
      what can you know of it, for heaven's sake!
How hard this winter afternoon, hard this winter night
  white as a starched shirtcollar,
with stench from my cells' depths where wastes have putrefied,
  like frost on stale snow in an abandoned jar
aloneness grows within the understanding,
oh how can you think of leaving me all by myself,
      how can you think of it, for heaven's sake!
Like the membraned hard yolk shrouded in shrivelled white
useless solitude clouds my red cells' walls each night,

the engendered void finds no sweet fulfilment by moonlight,
as on ice half-empty egg shells crack and creak
in the wind of your going my stiffening atoms break,
 oh do not punish me so for being myself,
am I not near to breaking tomorrow's dawn?
oh how can you think of leaving me all by myself,
   how can you think of it, for heaven's sake!
Over my days I pulled on humility's secret,
 as onto a corpse white socks and shirt,
wool at its crotch, bared manhood ripening
 like a rich fruit, a white worm half-hiding it,
on the tree of un-being assaulted by death's frost,
 its ready great veiny fruit of flesh warned that it must
shrivel, till board-hard pallor bring down the axe.
Oh what can you, little one, what can you know of death, my love,
   what can you know of it, for heaven's sake!
Fog's cottonwool stops the flared nostrils of dead autumn,
a severe kerchief of grey stubble binds up its chin,
dusk's green eyelid slides over the sky. All's done,
for my comfort nothing but God's penny sun.
 Fog, fog, corpse fields, carrion stubble, where cornstalks sigh
the scale-leafed baytrees mount awkward guard upon
those who have no second death to die,
weeping stags flash across the dead meadows,
 snuff-coloured fawns cry after a mother
  like all living things,
on sugared putrescent wounds
livid-breasted fevers suckle their many ravenous children,
the days cough up into the night sky pustules of blue stars,
dream-flowers unfold across hearts their tendrils of phlegm,
distended man-eating flowers choke on their fill of blood.
Oh what can you, little one, what can you know of death, my love,
  what can you know of it, for heaven's sake!

Because it is winter, it's winter, dear love,
because it is winter, keep faith above all,
because it is winter, it's winter, dear love,
because it is winter, hold dear the impossible.
Yet winter's staggering hosts shall melt away, their bony
horses carrying off piebald corruption grinning,
its hord disperse utterly, blotched nags neighing shrilly,
arrows through their necks, already into thunder dissolving.
The Happy Arrow shall pierce Giant Horse winter,
greying upon its knees it will break into song.
Blessed are they who go in fear of death
and, surviving, do not live to whimper in horror!
The Hand shall plunge Steady Spear into winter's white breast.
It shall fall headlong, lie prone, possessed;
on Deadly Spear trembling soft flowers shall sprout,
in resinous wounds deep grass rise fragrant.
Because it is winter, it's winter, dear love,
because it is winter, keep faith above all,
because it is winter, it's winter, dear love,
because it is winter, hold dear the impossible!

And yet, yet to stand erect, to hope
for the Ultimate-Impossible, the Flame-Immaculate.
No, it cannot be that huckster death should deal out our fate!

Mary-Ann the fairest, once upon a time
Gathering blue cornflowers, went through a cornfield,
Gathering blue cornflowers, wreathed them in her hair,
Wreathed them in her hair, to wear her joy there.

You flower of the closed throat, lark of the iron tongue,
you dark harp, tiny mute goldfish,

you star of the deep seas, in your heart fearful,
oh in your innocence, what things you sing!

> Up, still up towards heaven was the girl yet gazing,
> Lo, there a bright footpath from the sky descending,
> There a flouncy white lamb prettily comes tripping
> Who between his curled horns sun and moon is carrying,
> See, a clear star shining on the white lamb's forehead,
> Both of his ribbed horns bear, see, a golden crescent,
> Two bright burning candles stand on each side of him,
> Fewer hairs his fleece has than the stars studding him.

Don't speak, don't speak, my lips turn blue,
I have seen the lustrous white lamb go,
upon me the Star fulfilled its fate,
and out of pain I trace the rainbow.
Like a meteorite arching on fire overhead
my throbbing body sparks with silver pain,
through my cells spreads like night mist a wordless void,
agony aches for release in the Great Ignition.
Upon me the fate of man fulfilled itself,
a great knife turns singing in my heart,
in primordial soil spins a red-hot knife,
the iron smokes, sizzling with meat.
Not in make-believe, poor love, but in suffering,
not in my suffering, but in our loneliness together am I burning,
till the last nova explode in the heavy radiance
of the bloodspray's luminous veil, and dissolve in rainbowed silence.

> Then the flouncy white lamb spoke thus to her, saying:
> —Be not frightened of me, Mary-Ann, fair maiden!
> There is a place for you in virgins' company.

I could take you to them, if you would come with me
To be a holy virgin in the choir of heaven,
Within their godly ranks you'd find room among them,
I'd put into your hands the bright key of heaven,
At the cock's first crowing to woo you I would come,
At the second cockcrow I'd in marriage ask you,
At the cock's third crowing away I would take you.


What is this I'm saying! Mother, heaven help me,
I would take you there, if you'd come with me quickly.
I'd feed you from my mouth, if you but came with me.
As the dove feeds its young I'd feed you so gently,
your feet which feel the cold in a wool blanket I'd swathe,
on your soft veined shoulder with my warm mouth I'd breathe,
laughing, with soft water I would wash your hair,
once again my shoulderblade you'd scrub with cold water,
I'd bring home a lemon, the fire I'd make ready,
working at its bright grate all day I'd be busy.


Heaven help me, mother, heaven have mercy on me,
tell me why you bore me, if only to suffer?
I bleed, I am soft with bruises, mother, I am so far away, so lost,
lost bird, lonely star, an orphaned wound.
Like the bank-manager's maid next door, I would make my bed,
        make it up at morning, in the evening turn it down,
pay the rent, tidy up, buy bread,
        and in the splintering solitude I would talk aloud.
I open, and close again, the cupboard; I might decide to light a fire,
        but my stove is colder than the hands of the Sunday dead,
discipline isn't enough any more, when there's no one to care,
        shadows thicken behind my brow, grow beyond my head.

Across my wide room dinosaurs lurch to their feet,
        they creak towards me at night, heavy heads staring,
vagrant meteors crash into my forehead, fever-driven
        in dreams armoured reptiles give me suck, full teats quivering.
Heaven help me, mother, heaven have mercy upon me,
tell me why you bore me, if only to suffer?
I'm like an orphan, and such pain, mamma see here the pain,
with your calcified yellow hands smooth sleep over my eyes again.

Your hands like yellow goose beaks, like marigold petals,
like webbed feet of geese, plucked chickens, flames of candles,
like gilt woodcarvings, old postcards, flushed tiny fishes' hue,
like weathered roofs your hands, God help me, I have forsaken even you.

    Weep for me, mother, let me hear in life,
    Hear in life how you'll weep when I have died!

Weep for me, mother, weep, weep for your daughter,
let me hear in my lifetime how you would mourn me!
Oh mothers, why can't you give joy when you give life also,
why must you bring forth life only for sorrow?

    —Daughter, my daughter! You, my flower garden's
    Tender honeycomb swelled by my first bee-swarm,
    From the tender honeycomb yellow-gold wax came,
    From the yellow-gold wax smoke's earth-hugging form,
    Smoke's earth-hugging form, its heaven-piercing flame!

Weep for me, mother, weep, in my lifetime mourn me,
mourn though I'm still alive, later on deny me,
weep for me, mother, weep, don't say it's all for nothing,
let metal shroud the sky, let smoke rise covering

the heaven-piercing flames, earth-lacerating knives.
Down from heaven to earth a yawning crevass dives,
robber white lamb, of you my heart goes in terror,
sidereal lice gleam where stars crawl in your hair,
as the wet flanks of seafish are covered with hard scales,
even so is your shape disguised by asteroids,
you Resplendent Robber, you Pious Manginess,
from vertiginous heights comes Shambling Ornateness,
Frilled and Beribboned Bier, you Ravenous Carrion,
you Foul Fiend of legend, with gold crescents for horns,
Black Ram who descending sets up a harsh bleating,
sun and moon equally for a mask carrying,
Sparking Sin, a spike-gilled gory and bloated fish
greedy for the pale salt seas of human flesh,
Insatiable Curse, echoing Hunting Call,
Opaque Word, the Sweet Lamb's bleating has proved deceitful,
you take soot from candleflame, you befoul our hearts,
Ravager of Wholeness, Dispenser of Wants,
still do I see you there, walking luminously
following heaven's grassy sheeptrack in a sunray,
each night a moonlit path warns me of your coming,
through my uneasy sleep frolicking and prancing
along my days' paths, you, advancing dressed in white,
step up to my bed where I lie blinded by the light,
like a lantern swinging around a hillpath's steep bend
relentlessly into each of my nights you descend.

Release her, release her from your enthralling gaze,
speak not with your seducer's tongue
fire-tailed star!
Return to your high trail of heaven,
put out your lights, blow out your candles

white lamb so fair!
Better far better the celestial meadows,
better far better fragrant celestial grasses
for your grazing!
Better far better that you upon soft curling cloud,
in the celestial fold's knotless smooth straw,
full-fed lie sleeping!

Do not lust after her you dusts, roots, and avid salts,
do not lust after her you saps, imperious insects,
all tiny earth-lozenges, beetles, larvae with humming motor,
soft machinery, scissors, and saws of frail translucent matter,
do not lust after her, odours, slimes, bacteria, greedy entities,
cosmic worlds, microcosms, known and unknowable forces!
Your hormones, nervous systems, laws pulsing through the molecule,
uncomprehending may yet still sense that it is impossible
to share my apportioned solitude.
Your minute intelligences, sinew-tissue, sucking stings, living material,
the claim to common life of your tongueless palate, your teeth-wall,
your bodies' delicate veining, their cell-walls' hope, shaping fires,
may still understand my heart, human yet akin to yours,
and pity me in my desperate want.
Genitalia of flowers, stars' orbits, lungs of creation,
pivots of ores, you vases moulded about the soft organs of insects,
you beetle eyes, from which no tear can ever come,
do not debase with your dry lust
my last hope, whose nature you can never discern!

Oh I cannot live with heart so forlorn!

A man takes his broken heart into a tavern
to drink himself under the table,

cries into his beer and chokes upon
the paper memories which stuff his soul,
suddenly it's blood rising in his glass,
and the coughing chrome-beaked syphon,
napkin, table, chair at odds with space,
the orchestra circling leaves the ground it's on,
like dogs in an earthquake the fiddler's yellow tool sets up a wailing,
with highnoon bright horn the trumpeter flies like an archangel,
the yelling drunk sets a course for nothing,
sees tomato-coloured birds from clouds of noise down tumble,
sees demons by the dozen climb ropes of smoke,
blotchy-dugged, bald-limbed, coupling in the murk,
watches the blur-faced ghost of the waiter, hears his croak
and senses poison in violets of scented plastic:
things have broken loose, are from me slipping,
no disciplines hold any more, order flies apart,
the world's rivets are sure no longer in their seatings,
devils busily divide my wounded heart,
with its starry cock a church spire flies aloft
like an arrow of stone and pierces the moon,
noise slaps back like a branch, memory is lost,
from my side nightly blood flows when my ribs open,
I lounge among stars, from beam to beam of light leap grasshopperlike.
Yet the dissolute world like a flock into the fold I drive before me,
my faith is my dog, back and forth nuzzling the flanks of things with a bark,
and atoms, the straggling herd of parts, rustle into a whole again,
no, chaos cannot destroy me, cannot destroy me.

Your eyes always sober me again, and love's passion
timidly given, food for the starving, nourishes me.

In my garden a presence stirs,
It is a sable dove who whirs
Snapping my flowers' heads, and cuts
The tops from my rosemary shoots.

Why do you speak, dear love, why, why speak of the black dove?
He flew away mocking, funereal scavenger, dismal bird, robber bird.
Why do you speak, dear love, why, why speak of the black dove?
A shot rang out: the flowers and rosemary have to bloom in blood.

In my garden a presence walks
And its shape is a black peacock's,
His tears run as he buries eggs deep,
It is he makes my flowers weep.

Oh dry your eyes, weeping flowers, no more lament,
though he come in mourning the peacock sang in vain,
weep not, poor sweet-smelling ones, rejoice in the event
and let the peacock in his sorrow screech again.

Someone's stirring in my garden,
He has the shape of a black swan
Who snaps with splayed feet my green shoots,
Tramples them with gold-scaled boots.

In me as in a plant recurs life's cycle, little heart,
as in a plant cells open along its hairy stalk, fibrous aspiring nerves
                                    and sinews,
delicately traced green vaulting, fluffy clusters,
so in me immortal life branches in resplendent hope,
out of me flower your unendingly fertile heavy-blossomed heartbeats,
your kisses bloom twice over on my overgrown trellis of care,

vainly come those others, slithering, baffling, in vain gnaw at me,
in vain tear at the immensity of my life, vainly breed
about my great life the many monsters, ferrets, wanton freaks,
bristling hairy caterpillars beslobber me with dragging beds of slime,
a weeping death's-head moth swoops on sticky stumpy wings,
the horned venom-injecting beetle in his armour, a murderous
                              desolation of squeaking tentacles,
bird-beaked mares, whinnying elves, fishes with incandescent nipples,
gold-toothed ulcers, bleak birds, bellies where eyes goggle,
vultures gilt-gizzarded, ears sprouting legs, a head from which spin
                              away rolling eyeballs,
bell-tailed mice, a booted puss stamping with spurs at heels,
cunning squids float past, or lurk stuck fast to marble tables
bleary-eyed, in the octopus hoverings of the signboards'
                              neon-green rhythms.
Untainted, little heart, we tremble together in the strong vortex of sins.


    Someone's stirring in my garden
    In the shape of a black falcon,
    Heavy as a calyx of gold,
    And sinking knee-deep in the ground
    With his gold spurs at it hacking,
    He shrieks to himself while crying,
    Where he treads comes the blood gushing.


The black falcon was pierced by an arrow,
once more brightly my garden bloomed,
hyacinth and rosemary are as fragrant
as the universe in the palm of God.
Only you may water my flowers,
above your heart you alone may pin them,
you the only one among the living

in the teeming flux of being,
only you on the whole horizon of suffering
taking on forms of plant, beast, star, and woman,
you alone whom creation has long been saving
to shape me, you the exclusive one,
to prove the world to me, making
you a dreamer, wise, and handsome,
you alone, there's nothing you cannot build,
like worker brigades in the empty acres,
constructing houses, a bridge, a road,
you can bring forth even fruitful silence,
my human void you alone can fill.
You alone can weave such stuff around
my loneliness that I share with you, as life clothes the cell.
You alone make me comprehend
that against death only twice-one can stand,
that in mere living is no merit, no aim
if there be no one to whom the heart can turn.
My only one, through whom I came to learn
that each who lives is a unique person,
not like the dead into last rigours frozen,
but bound together by love's interest and passion.
Existence is no mere mound of numb matter,
frost-covered, weed-tangled, from the earth growing
like the dusty rubble of some bombed quarter.
Hunger binds all things together.
Thus the world is made of married insufficiencies,
in completeness are dependence and desire mutual,
from stars to humans, flames to fishes
runs a chain throbbing in constrained survival.
This too I say, that you will bring my end,
if once my beauteous captivity you unbind.

If you accept the bribe of un-being,
my life also into death's trawl you'll fling,
like a deep-sea fish, flat and tiny,
hauled from the far-down splendid nightcity,
like a shelled egg holding together hardly,
in societies of flowering squid circling drowsily,
an electrical fever lights it brightly.
Like a red cherry it hangs from the twig of silence,
around it flash the green leaves of fish,
it can know happiness, but remove it and at once
between its teeth it will shed its organs,
veiny and welling greasily forth,
gills and stomach gushing from its mouth.

If your death should cast me out upon the air,
from off your bough of captivity tear
me, happy captive though I be there,
though I be the homeland of your future,
like the fish I'd emerge from far under,
which pain turns inside-out in its despair,
because alone I cannot hope, and by
myself alone, can neither live nor die.

[1956]

# Man imposes
# his pattern
# upon a dream

The torrid land is suffering,
man's awareness is beginning.
Duckweed shrivels in the fever.
All that was is gone for ever.

Now voracious instincts dwindle.
Only veined cellophanes rustle.
On its ribbed stalk, like a green bat,
the pumpkin leaf flutters its rag.

Within also, in a glassy mass
fused by the fire of consciousness,
is that which sprang up once, as dense
as weed, from depths of existence.

But nurtured hope learns to aspire,
as corn grows on the atom's fire.
Sober hormones nurse the hope:
its cause is mine, I'll not give up.

When all's said, man decides alone,
silence gives laws that are its own.
So much more than mere beast is man,
he'll grasp what frees him when he can.

The male locust makes charnel love,
losing life, he hands on enough.
Needle-lined angle-jaws, double rowed,
ripping his organs, the assured

female will devour the male,
her mouth's saws criss-cross and impale,
spiked bow bent in triangle head,
her heart the victim of acid.

Now this is how I stand to you,
giving all, making you fruitful
by consciousness, yet gobbled up
by you, my man-eating epoch!

Hot bloodclots by the sun are made,
where the tree slops its coolless shade,
the fresh green of tender parsley
casts a russet lacework near me.

The fledgling geese peck in the yard,
fat, shiny, yellow lumps of lard,

skin gritty with feather pimples,
their grease breeding volcanic moles.

A knife glints over them, concern
is poised above me, in my turn.
My throat cannot be slit by pain,
I grow, transcend, render it tame.

Shrivelled Evanescence cowers,
Mourning for its old psalter serves,
on a wrought-brass crucifix its
finger, like a green lizard, sits.

My small daughter runs to and fro,
pleased with her dotted ball, it's blue.
Yet her small soul carries within
outlines of the human pattern.

Strange words, sweet sounds she lets fall
shaping desires clear to all.
She plays, cries, grows, laughs, climbs,
under the steel girders of time.

So might our age be re-made to
a human pattern, once rescued.
Already as life's embryo has come
the blind, hermaphrodite atom.

In a deck-chair my mother's sleeping,
on the lawn her wings are breathing.
She thinks up for us in her turn
dreams made to a human pattern.

Studded are her gnarled feet with sores
that flowered on stone laundry floors,
dream-roots bearing the tree of sighs
and pain-budded boughs implore the skies.

The slate roof swelters up aloft,
and the metal-crested eaves trough.
Green walnut coolness on my body,
summer's sulphur blaze choking me.

One blood-bellied yellow instant
is the poison-calixed Sabbath.
Wine and soda-water stand upon
my table. I take no absolution.

[1955]

# On the margin
# of my years
# in suspended
# animation

Talk too much, then did I?
Will dumbness be my fate?
For my seer's heart, worry?
Has drought dried up my throat?

What skeleton armies have
by my star-fate been summoned?
Have they devoured my faith?
Is my face a gravemound?

[1963]

# Firelily
# in the
# night

Firelily in the night,
I do not believe in the mockingbird's luring,
do not believe in worldly-wise wrongdoing,
do not believe in man's sinning,
in this tremendous summer a madness throbbing,
firelily in the night,
I do not believe in the mockingbird's luring,
grey-fur giant moth in electric loneliness wheeling,
its grey star to God's smile adding,
firelily in the night,
plant creatures' green lameness,
green exhalations and plant darkness,
manic worm-sadness spilled from each other's
fibrous silences, giant petal tatters,
green excitement, mare on heat above
with ardour's bloody vulva reflex-love,
mockingbird-lips' fluttered voluptuousness,
firelily, tell me of your aloneness,

firelily in the night,
I believe so much in man's miracle,
in something good, something beautiful,
some purpose man's called to fulfil,
firelily in the night,
moon in the walnut tree's green tangle,
moon in the green method of the walnut's tangle,
firelily at the rim of lightning-light's circle,
firelily, whore for a night of star-earth,
green thorned stalk-marrow's outward flaring mouth,
from shadowed emptiness prayer ascending,
tiger roar, bloody whitemetal casing,
green palm's erect flame-sexuality, higher
a yellow lizard-comet lashes your brain of fire,
its huge battleaxe lays open the universe,
its wind's swish downward to the bowels of hell,
firelily in the night,
in this tremendous summer a madness throbbing,
over my heavy heart licks a comet tail,
like jellyfish tongued-in by a killer whale,
like corona-squids' flaccid tangled tentacles
down on my head loosing its laced light-whorls,
some savage angel is weeping in the night,
in an outer world fluttering out of sight,
some blind devil in blind space stamping,
cornets and cymbals in sin to ashes burning,
world-generating stallion, whinneying, called
his mate, kicking hooves back at the blue eye of God,
from the blue eye of God the flame sheets down,
in heaven's howling storm of sparks I drown,
up there roars the Gilgamesh sky-bull,
no one to slay him, no one upon whom to fall,

moon's fire-rainbowed tumescence rises
pouring into space immense slag fires,
in this tremendous summer a madness throbbing,
firelily in the night,
earth trembles, the sea is crawling to the moon:
glutinous renewal, amoeba maelstrom,
in this tremendous summer a madness throbbing,
firelily in the night,
beneath the contorted walnut tree's stone bark
lilies' fires burn holes in the dark,
overhead the dream completes the age of stone
with the walnut tree's cement Laocoön,
down upon lilies screws its meshed stone-muscled
stone-snake vortex, their wounds blood-marbled,
barbed swordfish lance, evil purpled hydra,
leopard's spot avid for raw flesh she-star;
above foundation root-weave, plant's rib-casing,
plant's green wheel-arms, the bloom-blood sobbing:
firelily in the night,
I do not believe in the mockingbird's luring,
like dragon's eyelashes, darkening bands
of leaf-shadow fall on our tight-clenched hands,
I do not believe in the mockingbird's luring,
firelily in the night,
wakeful silence-shedding catafalque candle
lighting up our watching heart's vigil.
Mankind must not burn up apart
like firelilies in the night.

[1963]

# Gold twig
# of past time

Raising his faint-gold bow, so gently brown stillness
back and forth played upon the slack strings of silence.
With crouched mourning beetle's sombre body he stands
over silence lifting his two red-palmed blue hands,
and from the golding great stable voices clamour
joining with his swelling lilac-toned viola:
with web-foot patterings, with clicked beak-chatterings,
with bloody shiverings, with bubbled chirrupings.

Roaring redly, daybreak's greyish slaverings run,
from its distended teats drip the soft dews of dawn,
towards light's pink nipples plant-fingers reach for milk,
trumpet-eyed flowers tilt clustered faces to drink,
petal mugs with dew-milk glisten in every vein,
life's blind herds of jellies gather in light's soft rain,
near Eyes of the Virgin spotted-winged butterfly
the tiger of brown moods is lapping harmlessly.

The little lake will stir, the little fish will wake
mouthing at its surface with leathery shell-face,
each gill's small medallion closes and reopens,
inside flower also tiny tight ruby fans:
the minute gill-pinions' feathery red nosegay,
panting gently to live, fanning sinuously.
A grass-snake wriggles past, hissing modestly,
blood-rooted fins flicker and flash nimbly away.

The earth made a turn; stillness, wings wide open,
struck up with his music's velvety purple tone,
in all directions surged lilac viola-sound,
in brownly yawning caves it stirs deep underground.
To and fro the bow, in delicate red fingers,
coaxing mists to rise high as the brains of flowers:
this the bow's way in the hand of the brown angel,
stickying the meadows with baby calves' spittle.

Could this have been childhood? One twig of it only,
one thin gold twig only from torment's tangled tree.
I could call it tear tree, shudder tree, grieving tree,
a haunted tree it was, growing in fear's country.
Lashing its bleeding leaves against the tear-wet rock,
with such heavings, writhings, until its gold flaked off,
the sombre tree suffered no Cinderella twig,
a twig that was to fall in the man-eating bog.

Somewhere you are lying, my twig, little tower,
like my fawn-time fallen, like a queen bird's feather,
like gold knees of Buddha where jungle creepers grow,
like the skull-thorn jutting from a rotting rhino,
like a king's sword in a swamp which drank a people,

like a ringed shin-bone in an earth-covered castle,
like a life-like corpse on a salt-crystal altar,
like a hair of God on the drooping world's shoulder.

My childhood's envelope, my moulted stiff coffin,
lying on the path from time past, a lizard's skin
quite empty, jaws agape to the throat, with scaled skull,
reflected light bloating its body to the tail,
skin embossed with a face and horny bubble-eyes,
its feet like crumbling gloves with empty claw-spaces.
Like cellophane, the past's membraneous shed-wrapping,
cracks, pores, creases, show its former cell-flowering.

There it hangs, rattling, on the dark crags of my night,
the Milky Way, perhaps God's shirt of woven light.

[1964]

# At childhood's table

I am thirty-seven. Not yet old enough to be wise and well-ordered like the plants, the animals, the celestial bodies, and not so young any more that I should not always be thinking about death. And yet I have lived always with death. There she sat at my childhood's flowered oilcloth table, bone wings enfolding her, giant bat, ancient ark's huge hull-frame aground upon time's crystal tower, and the shadows of her wide-pored bones latticed our house and our larva-tender hearts. And I would look at the loose brown lace stitching together her world-bubble skull, and the starry cavity within her flapping rib-cage. Or in an undergarment of roots, mossy-eyed and mould-haired, she would sit on the blood-pimpled autumnal cliffs of my adolescence, and oil-reeking wrecks of bombers hung from her stalagmite mouth's cave, metal-veined fabric wings, polished huge insect eyes, bits of radios, and machine-gun barrels, and she was staring out at the gold-lashed god-eyed sunflowers that staggered in the fog. And she lay there, a waxen rose growing out of my mother's womb, in the tiny blue coffin, a frozen tear under the veiling lace, in my never-effaced ice-flowering contemplation's winter window. And she lies there with her muddy bones, roots tying her hands down, trees of soil in her never-ending lungs, toads hatching in her jaws, with her starred porcelain spine stretching across all of my thirty-seven years, with swollen bare bones growing back to the beginning of time, and her skull ballooning like never-bursting soap bubbles over the miraculous strata of the future, on to the eternal parturition of the universe.

I was born at Bia, a village near Budapest, and lived there till I was twenty. A delight or sorrow to my dear parents? Which, I don't know. I cannot ask my father any more. Too soon the planet's stomach broke down his perishable flesh. The time of questions had not yet come and the age of answers was too far off, when with his wildfowl bones he went down into the fermenting ground with white socks on, his hands bound round with a rosary, a twig of dewy rosemary between his palms. From under porcelain-skinned halfclosed veiny eyelids he fired gold questions into my tearless eyes, then pulled over himself the old mat of earth, and turned away his foam-flowering head. He lay silent.

I could go to the wintry cemetery at the village's outskirts, under the Christ shadow of its carp-scaled wintry-barked elder trees, rotted frozen chrysanthemums, clumps of mucus Michaelmas daisy, rust-marbled lacy hemlocks, snowy iron-hard turfed spaces, scattered rooster feathers, human bones working their way up out of the earth, coffin splinters, shredding wreaths, and ragged filthy shrouds, and I could shout down into the frozen ground. Or I could descend into cold matter like a magician. But I am not going to disturb him who is dead. Only the dead can talk with the dead. I believe in death and I do not believe in annihilation. Some day it will be me lying in the slimy and mouldering wearing-away mud pit, earth teeming with the dead of millions of years; I'll be holding his blessed bone hands, and we'll be talking together. Then I shall ask my father, was he weeping for me? For I have cried much for him. This I know: the dead speak with one another. The earth is loud with bone voices, choruses, and songs. The

world below isn't silent! I'll talk with him and everyone else there. I shall
signal through the gelatinous fires, heaped with the seething dead, to the
globe-crust's far side. At a sign from my bone finger the whirling flame-
octopus will part like the sea, and I shall call down through the flickering
hot cleft, and bone hands will wave back at me. I shall talk on with my
father for billions of years, and ask all of them there about life. The poets
and the soldiers and the peasants and the bricklayers, the women and the
kings. Those cast in gold, those crushed into the ground, those kneaded
into mud, those petrified into marble. For only they can speak truly about
life. About death, only the living.

I cannot ask my mysterious lonely mother. Whenever I look into her
incandescent secret and star-shadowy eyes, I leave off asking. Should I ask
her now why she bore me? Why nursed me? Washed for me? Should I hurt
her now, she who can be made to grieve? Sons shouldn't trouble mothers
with questions. And never insist upon answers. Then too mothers' tears
are as rare as peaceful dreams. The goodness of mothers makes them tell
lies. They never speak of that which hurts, and their love makes them silent.
Did she know that it was a star she carried in her womb, that she was press-
ing her small nipples into the mouth of a dragon-infant? Did she know that
she was the chosen one? That in space above that body of hers able to
receive the glad blessing and gestation, a blood-coloured angel hovered,
with huge red-hot legs singeing the dark reed and green moss-mucus
thatch, beflowered with snakeskinned bone-lace wreaths, his flame-wings
swathing the universe in sheets of light? That she was going to be one of
the family of stars, ancient mothers who gave birth to the universe and
birds?

I was an obstinate and wilful lad, nervous and always planning things,
sulky and making ready to save the world. Inhibited and wild, dreamy and
all the time in love. Always wanting something different. Always pre-
paring for death. We were very poor and unhappy. Since then my mother
has gone to my brother's in Budapest. She sold up the house, dear child-
hood house, and even after that we were very poor. Now in my dreams

I am always at home. I see the moonlit wintry courtyard and the moonlit summer garden. And in my thoughts I always return home; I would like to throw myself down beneath the mulberry tree and melt into the earth, turn to earth. To be soaked up by the roots, by sucking grasses. To rustle in the mulberry tree's leaves, break out as moss on plum-tree bark. Looming among the dill plants, the poppies, the love-in-a-mist, I too am dill plant, poppy, love-in-a-mist. And swell among clustered mauve volleys of starry rocket-trumpets in the hooded green blister-beetle-devoured lilac bushes. To be the root-moustache of the familial faces, veil-fish tailfinny, to be gorgon-bearding and eyebrowing and copperwire-eyelashing the familial heads. To be the August wind's dry smile, tawny-owl hoot, owl-curse down chimneys at the homes of the laid-out dead. And to be the worm-headed wick flickering beside fragrant catafalques, primrose of light on mourners' faces. To be ragged king of the herdsmen, my greasy skull crowned with everlasting straw-flowers.

Yet how much I hated that house, that road beside the lake, everything and everyone who was at home! Hated! Or loved them? Tousled hair hung thick, wild-horse maned, to my shoulders; then for years I went cropped close like a convict. I used to roll in the grown-woman's hair-flowing early summer fields, on hillsides sticky with dandelions' milky crushed stems, glassy, rubber slavering, hemlocky, stinging nettly, sumachy, fermenting, with rusting pots, sharp plate-sherds, broken fryingpan handles, cracked glass lamp bellies, copper-ribbed lamp cylinders, wires, among rotting, puffy, wire shaving-brush moustached and long-dead cats, green, pitted, mouldy, trampled-upon glove-like toads, dead stripped-breasted chickens, discarded wreath frames, rain-sodden gold-lettered wreath ribbons, chicken bones, skulls of chicks, violet resinous pigs' shelly hoof-joints, suppurating hog bristles, dry splintering dripstone bone-spokes and marrow-bones long since sucked hollow, hacked-about glazed inner bone-sponge cow knee-joints, gold-scaled chicken legs like gripping bases of ancient candlesticks, bloated, fraying-skinned at the soles, mushroom pillowed, fleshy dead-clawed, puckered, gold-fan gooselegs, spattered eyes, and greatcoat-buttonhole nostrils in bloody birds' heads, ducks' heads saw-edge beaked and yellow-skinned in the blossoming putrefaction, in the rubbish-heap flowering, in the stink bliss, the bee and wasp buzzing, butterfly mouldering, dragonfly maddening intoxicated plant life's floodtide.

At the bird-calling, dog-barking, goose-cackling, hen-clucking, rooster-cock-a-doodle-dooing far end of the village, I used to sit deep in thought beside the lake with its green-pimpled grey-scabby cucumbers, huge beanpod bullfrogs, glutinous corduroy snails paddling on whitish saliva, with puckered virgin-mouthed leeches, horror-eyed water-beetles, eaten-away furry field-voles rotting from ringed metallic tubular tails, mudfish with coalbright skins and eyes coal-dust glinting, flame-freckle glass-glove crested newts, space-station waterspiders, velvety shellbacked horse-ticks, butterflies in mourning, dragonflies in widows-weeds, tiny little male dragonfly larvae-grubs on the banks of the brook—with all kinds of creatures crawling, writhing, flying, jumping, swimming, hissing, seething in the sedge, the reeds, the rubbery wreaths of bulrushes. I used to lie in the demented summer's blissful roar, plant and animal rustling, echoing, clattering, drumming, swishing with the milliard destinies of crickets, locusts, grasshoppers, in the love-ferment of red poppy, cornflower, teasel, ears of corn, in the blessed close feathers of the earth, under its crust's scintillating wings that stir susurrating in the pulsating light, in the gold-haze-ruffled, harp-sounding, green-smelling feathers; I used to sit beside freshly-dug graves, upon their heaped soil mixed with brown root-fibres, coffin crumblings, rotted clothes-tatters, pearl buttons, dry pumpkin-shells of big-balled skulls, spade-quartered bloody toads, the insects' red-hot discharges of white creams, and smelling of bayleaves, the aromatic mint, incense, mustard-seed, French marigold, ginger, luckynut, in the elder bush's fragrant shadow, the whitewashed doll-faced freshly touched-up gap-wounded vomit-blood hearted gold stone nailed Jesus, in the velvety stench of elder bushes, and with the universe's curdling whirlpool galaxies, fire-rings, red-hot fog-spheres, ropes of flame, blood whorls, gold saw-strokes in my heart.

I loved everything. Everything animal and plant, the invisible and the visible: the fluffy, the tegumented, with rhythmic air-passage exhalations, liver-equipped, the many-legged, many-winged, multiple-eyed, worms, spiders and their webs, cockchafers' metallic baytree-antennae, night-butterflies' cottonfern huge ears, the birds and roots, metals, crystals, salts, rocks, moss, and wasps' blue mossed bodies, crystal hedgehog-like corpse chins, the ice-bubble panting of catfish frozen into the ice surface and their yellow trailing snot-moustaches, woodpeckerings and tree-frogs' damp diaper rubber-wrapped groins pulsating, the trees' aromatic scaling ancient bark, water gullies, leaves of grass, green lungs of trees, their sun-meditating pinions, fibres, buds, leaves; the water, goose-pimpled with rain blisters, frothing, its roots in clear sources, green muscle-matted, self-begetting, womb of the monsters and ancestors; the hollow unsworded snakeskin sheath and the reptilian roots of creeper, the rust and the snow, the rain, the single-celled animals, and the mysterious wondrous blood, the domesticated and the wild beasts of the forest, the rot, the decay, the putrefaction, the swellings, the blissfully coursing lymphatic waters, and cows' white, mossy, rosy-rooted udders, the gold sex-acorn of flowers, their gold clitoris, the swollen plant skins, black-blue plant-blood stripes, blue umbelled insides of their wombs, gold-dusted love-proboscis, the bees' thigh-slung gold-sacs, flower-pollen pitchers of hair on translucent thigh muscles, the deer's snow-track of violet urine and the baby rabbit's rosy camel-nostrils; the toads, which resemble moss, bog, reed-grown mould, soldiers' blunt boots rotted away from the leg; the meteor showers and the earth, this indescribable smelling smell, earth's earthy smell, this oozing, dry, clayey, alkaline, limey, this boiling and frigid, soaked and summer-baked stuff, to bury the face in it, sprinkle my body with it, scratch it over my heart, to eat it, bite it, breathe it in, sucking, kissing, smelling, greedy for it, embracing it, this earth—our animal being's fire-hearth, female udder, lung-cave blistered, never drying-up mothering groin, whose milk splashes on the celestial bodies, the ancient curse and greedy graveyard of all our created things, ever renewing itself, the earth, the earth, the earth, into which some day I shall be absorbed also.

Only when my father got drunk, that's what I didn't like. And he was drunk often, my father—my father, gentle drunk, kindly drunk. Yet what I was most afraid of never happened. He never argued, never started fighting, never yelled, never chased us with the kitchen-knife or axe round the peeling-skinned and long-haired dwarf house, or the green carpeted moon-lit yard. He never chased us out into the angel-throng wrestling snowstorm or under the green-bile coughing November sky, so that weeping we would see his panting white bubblings—autumn rains with bloody dahlia fringes, soaked fowls, the dog grey with wet—him framed in the paraffin-lit amber cube. He just stood there with a blissful grin, plastermask grin, Greek tragedy grin, so that once I was sure he was going to pull aside from his face a painted papiermâché grin and laugh his youthful laugh at me, but he just stood there, grinning, all muddy, face, ears, nose, hands all covered with mud, bloody autumn's secretion. He was standing, arching his sprouting fern-hair eyebrows, peacock-tails of spun copper; just standing there smelling of mud, rain, tobacco, wine and sodas, of the city, of sweat, and rummaging in his old mud-stained briefcase for the city shop-cakes, like misshapen crustaceans: chocolate-coated crescent rolls all bent in his mud-covered palm, oozing green blood, flavours all runny, stuck together, sweetly sticky with clustered sugary roe-crystal grains; he stagge-red and lurched holding them out to us. Only once did he overturn the kitchen-table, the drawer sliding out with its porcelain onion-knob, scatter-ing over the floor pitted cooking spoons, well-chewed aluminum spoons, forks, and flower-patterned steel knives, and with great delight he very deliberately smashed the star-spangled white china greyhound which I had got from the Bia choral society committee for my part in *The Yellow-Buttoned Private.*

I would shiver: I liked to crawl into his bed. When he would let me. I could only lie back-to-back, or turn my face to his back, under the big sweaty feather tick; yet it felt so good to breathe in the father-smell of his soaked shirt, to dig my boy's cropped head into his back's deep hollow, to feel my eyelashes scraping the softened fibres of his old shirt and listen to the contented panting of his rattling half-lung, which spoke to me like an old dry forest. Waiting for dawn's first crowing, watching the way the gold lily of starlight slowly fades upon the embroidered face of the Virgin, the way dawn's tall skin-crested, blood-sac bearded, ambergris galley-beaked rooster's head peers into the room's wreathing galactic winter-fog, for we always slept with the windows open. My father was a huge man. His back on its right side was a boneless deep fleshy hollow, a mass of lilac scar-embroidery whose thick welts covered with wide flower-patterns the ribless, pancake flat, deflated balloon side of his body lacking a lung, like gold braid on long-ago hussar coats. That blue-stitched trough was the living grave of my childhood. Silent, motionless, not rising, not falling, maimed and soundless, half death, half cemetery. Yet pressing my ear to the moist, boneless, blue root-laced hollow, how happy I was listening to his unhappy body's shrill wheezes, rattles, bubblings, its pounding regular heartbeat, the harsh gurgling in the air-passaged wearing-out bubbles-branched half-lung, the whispering, fizzing ebb and flow of blood, the tortoise slow curved rib-movement, the wing-creaking bone feathers hinged to the flesh. Like the sea, body that could scarcely stay alive. Like over cave-networks encrusted with shells and snail-scaly earths, I would bend over his mysterious body, where vapours decompose, over icy waterfall-beards' wind bubbling, jetting, roaring into unknown dark caverns, flower-floored dripstone forests, grave-mossy bat-nests, subterranean oceans, where tiny eyeless white creatures growing eye-sensations over their bodies live on in the icy dark glitter.

My father was always coughing, spitting, sweating, hawking up, gasping. At such times his long transparent writhing nicotine fingers would grab at the air, like a harvester spider alighting on paper, or pearly-socketed long legs of a horse-mosquito torn out at the roots, caught in his terror, killed by shock. Then he would have a smoke and down a mug of wine. He was a bricklayer, then an office messenger, office extra—clerk, so called. After the war, bricklayer again, factory worker, dying in February, dead-in-his-prime defiant giant, epic-hero in marble on the catafalque, waxen plank slid into the earth, buried, bone-bound book written all over with sorrow, cosmic secrets, mould, rot. What did he expect of me? Did he believe in me? Was he scared of me? Was it redeeming he thought about, when he was going to make me? Did he comprehend that he was a mission-entruster, that he was a ransoming herald? That he was love's hugging golden titan-angel? That his earthquake-intoxication man-creating pleasure was writing the future in fire within the body opened to happiness? That in his being's shaping, vigorous, well-used painter's-palette-coloured raging fire-course, erupting lightfogs, world-fire swirling galaxy formations, that in the soft and bleeding hot-organed space the talking flame, the epic-creating secret waters, the singing matter was going to clot, break into billions of whole cells, and would grow? Some day I shall ask him, and he'll tell me.

I was small, a thin lad. Nervous, with a sensuous imagination, a child's hard-thumping heart. I used to do casual day-labour even as a little urchin, on the railway and the estate farm. With my sleepy staggering fellow workers, yawning and choking I used to roll up the green-skeletoned, drying-veined yellow-podded pea-vines in endless waves, fields of god's blood dawn-breakers, like dewy barbed wire, in huge coils, wet up to my navel with heavy-budded dew, dust stuck like a mask to my sweaty face; and tall silvery-branched thorn trees teased, pricked, pecked at me, like indifferent greedy birds at dying soldiers' flesh. I was always bleeding, muddy, sweating. And I yearned for the long-bearded, suddenly down-pouring, fire-toothed rain, when I could sit under the asphalt-barked elder bushes, soaked to the lungs, and could watch the squirming hermaphrodite savage kissing with the whole body of maddened marrying snails, white-worm raindrops seething across the dust, rain's frog-bubble creeping ascent, death's-heads on the casings of stuck-together mating graveyard beetles, their red-orange porous wing-shells, orange-peel eyeballs of animal glass standing up from their skulls.

I used to go out to hoe, earth up, rake vines over, fork swathes, bind sheaves, build ricks, carry chaff, heave sacks, snap corn-cobs, pick pota-toes. I used to load planks in the timber-yard, split boards with the power-saw, fell timber in the forest, build fences round the young landlord's walnut trees, dig up copses. And I used to go to lend a hand with the bricklayers. This I liked best of all. Tearing down old wattle-and-daub cottages, throwing the bricks up onto the scaffolding, wearing down the skin between the fingers to the red layer—the skin's pattern worn away like the stone's grain, and you could see the blood throbbing in the fingertips, like the heart of the chicken-embryo in the candle-transilluminated egg taken from the broodhen—cutting the loose-boned, spongy stone to aluminum smoothness, chipping sharp angles onto squared stone, cutting exactly down the centre of the thick blacklead carpenter's pencil-mark; stirring up the foaming, pale, greasy, just-warm mortar to know what water and sand to add, and sometimes cement, for good, proper, bone-binding mortar, in the bird-dense dawn, thinning down rich, greasy-skinned, plucked chicken-white mortar in the bottom of the mortar-box, to make it soft and just right like yellow foam, and useful like goodness; mixing in loosening mud, as it foams watching big black-skinned bubbles rising from deep in the sludge, like oceans' creature-miracles, to breathe in the mud smell of work, its stone smell, lime smell, brick smell, cement smell, plank smell, bricklayer's-hammer smell, tarpaper smell.

My parents sent me on from primary to senior elementary school. This was in Bicske, twenty kilometres from my home. The train taking me to Bicske took my father to Budapest. In the ice-crunching, white covered winter dawn, yellow rock-bulb moon's halo-ribbon tied around space, we used to trudge along with frosty faces, iced nostril-hairs, ice-straw eyebrows, breathing out white tongues of vapour like the damned. Above us the transparent corpse of dissected space sprawled from the world-island out to islands of other substances: wrenched-apart joints, bone growths, glimmering muscle-clusters, weary muscle-ribbons, ribs, steaming viscera, withered blue heart-valve shells, and the huge brain's yellow rind in the blood-rimmed skull-cavity, beside the sawn-off skull's top: moon with phosphorescent convolutions. But why did they accuse me of stealing when a purse with twenty pengoes in it was missing from the classroom? Because

I was the poorest, perhaps? For they humiliated me and shamed me, frightened me and threatened me, made me cry and never even said they were sorry. And why did we have to pay the forty pengoes, when it was one of my travelling schoolmates who smashed the train-window? Because I was small and unable to stand up for myself? Poor and afraid? Why do they have to make the poor pay for the sins of everyone else? I'll never forget the shroud-complexioned, silkworm-grub featured, arrogant ring-wormy necked, blue uniformed station-master, the humiliation of identification, the slowly rolling wheels of the train, for I had the urge to throw myself under them, to end it all! And how much shame and how much humiliation! At the estate's manor, at the bricklayer's, at school, with the older boys, in the village. Was I a madman or monster to them? With their what-does-this-guttersnipe-kid-want, this colt-haired idiot? Who could be chased away, shamed, be excommunicated, crucified? Only my hatred and disgust were growing, like the fluid in my chest during the war, growing fit to choke, to kill me, and they were already setting up the heavy candles for the dying from the church by my head ripened into an amber skull, and the priest was making ready to give extreme unction. And already he was coming silently across the snowy spaces of the village square ringing his handbell. Oh, father, mother, how much did you go through because of me?

Just to get away, away, away from here: from the land of hatred, from the land of curses, from the country of roots, from the empire of bloody chicken-heads, bone-blooming, mallow and lily flowering manure heap, to shed it the way the *libellula* turns into a diamond-skulled conqueror, to wriggle out of the puppy-fat furry damned skin-suit of larvahood, to crawl out of the gilled veiny layer of shelly armour, suffering horribly, convulsed from hovering in the air on triumphing lungs, relayers of lightning, and never again turning to look back at the fat, bloody shreds, veiny torn membranes, pale-pored torn envelope of yesterday, outgrown rags of childhood, strewn along the shore of the past. To be high like a star above the choked up, hairy marsh-covered, bone-framed, torment-feathered, curse-rigid, fish and frog moon-mouth cratered, lightless world. To be the herald of light and redemption. Now I shall go back to my native village and I shall run out to the snowflake, gelatinous sleet, dead autumn-flower cemetery, where black porous snow-slices lie slowly melting on top of the blue fungus-grown marble gravestones, like soaked pieces of bread, and the wooden crosses' gold inscriptions and silver dates are effaced by rain and snow, drawn close by mighty fog tentacles curling through the village; where pressing against rose glass and light-blue porcelain frames, the photographed faces, curly hair, moustaches, hands, neckties, shirt-fronts, tie-pins are slowly crumbling, sticking to the glass, curling, peeling off, cracking, wrinkled, weed-root penetrated, picked to pieces by the end of winter melting and the rain. I shall go out to the silent field of rotting wreaths, torn white crepe-paper-bandaged wreath-wires, frozen petalled flowers, bones lying in cindered mud, bare, wind-whistling poplars, acacias, sumachs, elder bushes, lilacs, crudely carved Jesuses not yet freshly white-washed, sorrowful faces of the Virgin green-spotted with death, marble crowns of thorns, rusty tin candle-holders, wet candle-stumps, to the graveyard at home, and I shall thump on my father's grave. I shall shout down through the soaked earth to my wet-boned root-aware father's youthful bones; I shall hammer on the enormous earthy root-door and I'll ask him: did he know about my anguish? Does he know about my fate and my work of song? Do his earth-dulled eyeballs look back through the fifteen years of earth, and does he see my anguished questioning face? I know he cannot answer me, for the law of earth and roots arrests his mouth—earth his tongue, his brain earth, his lungs earth, his groin earth, his voice earth, his thoughts earth. And I shall go to all the graves: the grassy hollows, the weed-sunken, the gravel-bordered, the magnificently marbled, the sumach-bushy, the rosemary-lunged, the liver-coloured, funqused gothic-charactered crosses of marble swallowed between ice-scale strewn grave-teeth like a frog's webbed feet protruding from the grass-snake's skin-cave mouth, those where fresh wreaths have been knocked over, the weed-fringed, some with black skeletons of strange plants; I shall visit all the graves and shall greet the dead.

I shall greet the dead, for we should greet every one of our departed. And I shall ask my grandfather: has his moustache overgrown the earth beneath its crust, like the root system of mortality, flowing over continents, beneath oceans, eternal phosphorescent meteoric moss? And I shall ask the girls: do they still remember the pursed kisses under the lilac bushes, the blushings and stammerings, the small rose-patterned perspiring palms, twisting, wandering, interlacing smooth tiny horns around and under each other like snails in love? I shall ask the boys: do they still remember the wintry forest stags, slowly moving behind the afternoon shroud-curtain snow and mist, which halted on the forested far side of the hill, went on again, stopped, from time to time putting their noses out into open snow-flake-space, blowing antlers of steam; making their way through our snow-covered childhood, in-love childhood's cuddled star-animals, like Jesus with his disciples to the mount of revelation, hill of mission, Jesus with his followers to the hill of crucifixion? I shall ask the married women, who were in love with me: do they still remember the fragrance of hay, the ones dying in the shadows on the village's Calvary Hill, the shadow crosses on the giant moon-breasted summer night?

I shall go knocking and pounding at all their graves, and I would pound upon every poor man's grave on this earth, on every poor man's grave on this green-bearded, blue-skinned globe, on those of my forefathers and ancestors, relatives, brothers and sisters; but I do not know the places where their bone-ends' marrow, spongy animal-bodies, splinter-bearded ancient bones, legs, skulls, spines, fell to pieces; I do not know the places where earth fills their teeth's cavities and where their hearts have dispersed within the lower universe. Their graves are not known to me; for time, memory, that which is written, take no account of the graves of the poor. They have disintegrated in forests, meadows, battlefields, are mouldering away within fortress walls, dusty ditches, under cartwheel-clattering highways, drying up in birds' stomachs, animals' stomachs, larvae's stomachs, fishes' stomachs, worms' stomachs, locusts' stomachs, mantises' intestines, bats' stomachs, bees' stomachs; they are powdered into the mortar of churches, absorbed by the root-mouths of root-brained trees, in the mouths of leeches, frogs, snails, and in the fatty cells of the earth, in the stomachs of snakes, and in the mucous dripstone-toothed stomachs of caves.

But where can I find the insect ancestors, fish ancestors, worm ancestors, primeval mammal ancestors, fox ancestors, bird ancestors, reptile ancestors, snail ancestors, moss ancestors, and plant ancestors? Where am I to find my ancestors' ancestors, the genesis ancestors, the battlefields, cannibals of long ago, bricklayers, herdsmen, woodcutters, day-labourers, serfs, fishermen, and soldiers? Where shall I find the first mothers, who have withered into root-tubers, the gnome-bearded primeval mothers, and the rest of them all, the world-creating wombed, volcano-pelvised, groin-bleeding women?

I would ask them: what did they know of the future? The humiliated and sorrowing ones, forced to perish and rot while still alive: did they think about me? But I cannot ask of every insect, bird, lynx and tree; I cannot ask every root, rock, shell, clod. I cannot ask the earth, though perhaps my voice would carry through every particle of this egg-shaped star's grand-child; but the flowering-for-eternity-wombed first mother, curled around life's gold organ, would give no answer. The earth cannot answer. Yet I shall ask it of the graveyard at home, waiting to receive me also. Then I'll go to all the houses, I'll stop at their doorsteps, I'll knock. I'll step inside and ask: Do you still know me? I've come home. Let me sit at your table.

[1964]

# Images
# of the
# night

*The day I wrote this the skies were clear,*
*And green boughs blossomed from the crags of Earth.*

Vörösmarty

MEN'S CHORUS

Avid, unregretting, bark-scented night!
Green boughs cannot pierce the night.
Roofs cannot pierce the night,
windows cannot pierce the night,
grave-stones cannot pierce the night.
Night of insect's fungus eye, of bird's bloody beak,
                                    of profound root world.
Why no glimmer from the stars' deep-sea flowers?
Why won't the consuming soft arms of space pull
open the pulsing corona-mouths of the carnivorous stars'
chiselled teeth-rows of a blind flower-skull?
Night, bear-loin smelling, plant-viscera lining,
                                    coal wing-root of bird.

Solitude cannot pierce the night.
The night cannot pierce the night.
Only the wakeful watch. Twined branches of waking thoughts
flower out of sight.

CHILDREN'S CHOIR

Mr Snail to his snailhouse took,
tucking all four horns inside,
swallowing eyes of poppyseed,
for he doesn't want to look.

Mrs Snail to her snailhouse went,
on two horns her gold gloves grew,
dew-bells on the other two.
She tinkles them for the silence.

Baby-girl snail is asleep,
with her tiny horns so slender,
in a shell-house just as tender
she snores on a cabbage-leaf.

WOMAN

Sleep like them, your vigil is dark,
for night's phosphorescent life you need not wake,
close the smokey pages of your musings,
fold over your mind sleep's shielding wings
lest, finding you facing existence alone
the night release upon you all its old and young,
coupling crocodiles, creaking, that churn
up the green bog into spray, turn

mud to colour with their breath, bubbled sperm, blood, tears,
great crocodile-claws clasping reptilian mothers,
kings of meat slavering upon females in heat:
lest the mating muzzles devastate your heart!

Do not day-dream through the years of white foam.
Cease your musing. Start on the song.
There is pollen on my lips, stardust on my eyelids,
beneath my cropped mane softly moan birds' feathers.
I will lay close against you,
just breathe into my hair that loves you
—sleep!

POET

No!
I cannot sleep!
I see images in the night!
I see images in the night, like a blur of cards shuffled
                                    in the devil's hand,
I see images in the night, like teeth erupting along the dry bones
                                    of the dead.
I see images in the night, like staring eyes of water-animals
                                    surfacing,
I see images in the night, like screens of judgement flickering!
I see images in the night: a hand leafs through the layered heavens!
Ah, has judgement overtaken me?
Ah, is this the tongue of terror licking over me?
Ah, does the sliding jaw of madness crunch me, like flowers
                                    or grass
in a cow's rosy mouth?

CHORUS

Fool, say what you see!

CHILDREN'S CHOIR

Sleep, like the beetles sleep,
like larvae and insects,
like grubs and ovules sleep,
like horned beetles' wombs,
sleep like the roots sleep,
like fissures and rocks,
like eyelids sleep,
and ears without shells sleep.
Sleep, sleep, sleep.

POET

I can see beneath earth's belly skin:
in the book of earth I read the future's strewn lettering of bones.
I see into the high stars' membraneous wombs:
I can see in unsighing crystals the clustering embryos.
I see how the future is surging out of the past,
the blackly billowing past.
Mankind, I fear for you.

CHORUS

Fool, say what you see!

POET

Mankind has died!
Sprouting over the shrunken, spongy moonscape of Earth, solitude
                              and
peace-without-man flowers, like buttercups on the corpse
                              of a soldier,
for Mankind has died!

CHORUS

Alas, what remained after the destruction?
After the Atom, Hydrogen, and Neutron?
Cursing and horror? Curses, horrors!
But who any more can curse? Who is left to be horror-struck?
Rotted cosmic debris, boiled slime of human blood?
The dwarf tree, struggling up out of human flesh?
The rock coated with human bone, like a white rash?
Or those few who remained?

MEN'S CHORUS

But who are the ones who remained?

NARRATOR

Are they the dead or the living? The dead were printed upon seared
rock, upon Earth's stellar structure, like fossil creatures' shadow-imaged
parchment wings, spinal cords, or downy jellied dot of seed; is the
human race only a memory of the globe, like the departed ages of crus-
taceans, giant mammals, dragons, or vertebrates? And shall existence
without man grow ever lonelier, the soundless sadness of a sigh be all
from the orphaned few remaining before the final annihilation?

Why has life laboured to give birth to man through the milliard years' ascent from gas, fire, rock, plant, and animal? What did it purpose with its ideals, with purity, goodness, liberty? With ideals worth more than life itself, preconditionings of life's worth and meaning?

This insect's-heart-sized planet, this Earth, among stars as big as whales' hearts, is it to go on turning *emptily* in solitude, an overgrown, desolate graveyard, Mankind's graveyard? Or shall Man once more teem in torrents from its tortuous, exquisite womb, blessed little primeval mother, tenacious re-bearer of Mankind? Shall Earth tumble on over and over about the sun-star's fire-spouts, like a lonely desert of bone, metal, and rubble, or will there be someone to trim and comb out its straggly green beard, to burnish its dulled and cataracted wandering ocean-glance, to smooth the death-wrinkles of suffering from its Earth-countenance, and shall the deranged Earth-skull ever again conceive meaningful human thought?

CHORUS

Speak out, tell of the images of destruction, of living tissue's rebellion!

POET

All life is violation, all plant and animal monsters not yet known, a breed of horrors, schizophrenic, bloated, stuttering, croaking, whining and songless, plant dodecaphony, animal surrealism, insect existentialism, bird atonality. The Earth and its waters are a wilderness of savage, disoriented, drooping plants and animals. One-winged birds, two-legged horses, horned eight-headed stars, myriapodous frogs, camel-headed shaggy spiders, beetlish squeaking giants, lung-flowers, blinking tree-trunk creatures, whooping plant-tangles, cathedral column wheat-ears, and pygmy elephants, Siamese-twin bears and hydra-headed vultures, unknown diamond-cylinder snakes, glove-like animals flowering into the air, gilt-lettered coffin beetles, large rainbow-winged fishes, blue-leafed freakish forests, lizardy flies with mossed-over clustered eyes, babies' heads on dragonfly wings, tattered giant bat-mothers, inflated dew-worms, great songbirds with insect probiscises, wonderously scaled death's-head-marked moth behemoths, wiremesh animals, dragon's shed crested pearly clothes, tulip forests, narcissus madness and lily wilderness, vertebrates of grass, fish-tailed goats, cows ulcered all over with udders, mouthless animal crystals, mushroom dinosaurs and lily-of-the-valley towers, scarlet plant-creepers like live arteries pulsing, eviscerated queen toads wearing thirty-four hearts beating upon their skin, green-bearded swallows, locust-headed yellow-hammers, horned-beetle skulled hares, windmilling flies and cymbal micro-creatures, harp-voiced snakes, starry brooms, fringed hoverers, lacey animal-shrouds, bell-voiced bats, porcupine princes, gold-coated rats, and slobbering beaver-men slowly overgrow Earth's ruins, covering the cities' strewn concrete, stone, iron, roofs and cupolas, the grey haired waters and the black air.

## MEN'S CHORUS

Alas, what remained after the destruction?
After Atom, Hydrogen, and Neutron?

## NARRATOR

Was anything of Man left on the space-island of death? Anyone left on this earthly afterwards, after dying once, to suffer on through the *other* life of victorious monsterdom, time of derangement, post-Man existence? And the strange, never-before-heard sounds of this monsterhood? Anything of Man left, whose heart dared go on beating?

POET

And everywhere nether-world and after-life sounds in this grim and nightful world! All is sightless chirruping, harp glissandos, metallic screeches, woodpecker pattering and lizard-throat flutterings, naked babes' whimpering and animal coughing, all is midnight screeching and bird curses, snake-lament and jackal music, stars' tears and gold flicker, all hippopotamus teeth chattering and fox howling, all parchment crackling and flat-foot flapping, all diamond scratchings and frog croakings, all primordial cacklings and bears' lament, all machine-rattle and gear-grinding, all plant thrum and bird-throat bleeding, all death-sweat and satanic knocking, all whinneying of horses put to death, all shuffling, whimpering, rustling, choked off scream and whale-wheezing, insect gnawings and bone cursings, burst-at-the-nape leather wings creaking, panted hysterics and soft ululation, volcano bubble and caterwauling, women's labour screams and waterfalling mineral crackle, child bawling and obscure secret clatterings, closing in upon the *new* silence, after the last, the soundless sound, the not-even-heard sound, as pain closes in around Man.

CHORUS

Then how did Mankind regain faith?
Were machines to bring Man forth?

POET

There live on still, in solitude, the self-mutating machines that have survived; beneath impenetrable glassy weed-forests in their mole-man made purple-lit tunnel warrens, in Earth's concrete entrails, in the depopulated cities' wilderness of skeletons and human rottings, in the scrapyards of culture and civilization, on Mankind's rubbish heap swarming with multiple-headed flies, all over this rubbish-dump world, here and there their lamps will glimmer, give off signals, send out messages. Large electronic machine-mice, machine-ladybirds, machine-foxes, machine-monkeys scurry, roll, perambulate, their hard eyes glaring on-off rhythmically, nodding, clacking, hobbling, crackling; photo-electric-eyed steel doors open-close in empty underground chambers, monumental electronic brains compute hysterically, confusedly, unable to stop living, electronic translators print out unordered, garbled words, whole languages; in the back of a laboratory looms a man of glass in lilac-pink luminescence, like a glass rose lit from within, his organs and nervous system phosphoresce, arteries and brain outlined in flickering red-blue-yellow-green circuitry like a giant translucent mosquito-larva; centred in a tunnel's star, a machine man clad in rigid light repeats over, ten, a hundred, thousand, million times his recorded text; self-reproducing electronic devices bring forth self-reproducers, and they again more new ones, new hybrid machines tinkling, crackling, whimpering, machine-mothers in labour are whining, drenched in oil sweat; machine horses whinny, machine monkey-mothers clasp to their rubber teats dead decomposing monkey babes, fur falling out, turning to jelly; electronic composing machines orchestrate man-horse whinny-symphonies, galactic oratorios, and blast out music into the night of shattered vegetation.

CHORUS

And what remained after the destruction?
After Atom, Hydrogen, and Neutron?

POET

The Earth, like a small child's submachine-gunned body, oozes blood, fire jets from its wounds, eruptions of metallic saliva, incandescent stone, rattling flame. Gold spittle drying on its face, ruby-phlegm frothing over forest-covered cities, the death-maned Earth discharges like an excited stud-horse: love's iron-flame-gold spurting, and within this mineral foam swamping the world drift the stiffening dead and the living foliage of time.

CHILDREN'S CHOIR

As if centaurs and fauns were catching at each other through
the groves that blossomed out of the dead.
As if songs of sirens were carried here upon the blind sea-wind.

MEN'S CHORUS

The day breaks.
What is daybreak to the world, when it is dead?

CHILDREN'S CHOIR

Is day breaking?
Why does night's bleeding sheath squeeze forth the gold-toothed
Sun?
That it may see Earth's green-charred amputation?

CHORUS

The day breaks!
World, when did you last see daybreak?

NARRATOR

To Earth, beneath fluffy close coatings of smoke and dust like furry hair over heads of flies, the Sun can hardly break through. Bluish-grey dim glow spreads over the desert landscape. Vainly it presents teats of streaky light to the sickly infant earth. On the ruins of the night huddle a group of men, watching over the dead world's corpse. A city once perhaps was here where stretches this ocean of stone-grass-bone-rag-board-wire. They sit about, stand, mutter, claw at the air and as abruptly snatch back their hands, shivering in rags white with frost. The rigid faces of some are coated with glazed red clay like a mask, on others white clay juts like the beaked helmets of medieval knights, with openings skull-like only for eyes and mouth. How long have they been standing about muttering, shivering, drying out, these who are outside of time or new in time? How long have they been waiting, and for what? What do the remnants of Mankind expect? The despoiled, the loveless, the songless, the carrion-eating, the orphaned Mankind-debris?

Above them the dark, malign wheeling of flurrying air's radioactive covering ragged shroud. And then comes a metallic swishing sound, and they fall babbling to the ground like primeval men, so fearful that earth trembles from their heartbeats, like a locomotive raging along tracked embankments. And the grey-blue cottonwool mummycloth of death winding the Earth around is slashed by a scalpel-lightninged metal star, a disked sphere of metal, a Saturn falling among them, but with belly of glass trembling faintly like an egg broken onto a plate. And it is alighting on the ruins with a hiss, churning up bone-dust, plant-whirl-wind, blackened blood-crusts, red ashes. And a music woven of bird-tones filters from the machine's body, wondrously, softly, with bird-cadences of an unknown stellar existence.

The Earth-desert men slowly raise their heads, and unable to feel horror any more, see strange jelly-armed machine-thorax creatures descending from the machine, hovering on wide butterfly wings, like hybrid offspring of polyp, cricket, butterfly, and transistor. And they flutter about them, with softishly large, mellifluous, darkly-purple moth-wing waftings. And suddenly a *human voice* speaks to them, as if from a radio. It calls out to them: For your sakes, happy few, we have pierced the Universe's searing stellar indifference; yet we may come but *once*, never again. Knowing the death agonies of the cosmic molecule Earth, we have come for those who remain.

CHILDREN'S CHOIR

And they count the remaining ones,
the happy, the hapless ones.

NARRATOR

Within the machine born of another star-mother, there is not room for all these from Earth. Two must stay behind, on *this* Earth, for the disk of happiness, new womb, metal blissful mother, can carry all but two.

CHORUS

And the Earth-desert men, their tears long ago run dry, bend their heads low and murmur among themselves, those smeared with red clay, those with white clay helmets.

NARRATOR

And then the poet takes his beloved by the hand, and steps aside from the group of bleeding clay. He looks about him at the desert of ruins, and looks up at the death-furred sky.

POET

Here, for you, Mankind in shadow, we shall stay.
We stay here, we step out from the group of bleeding clay.
We preserve the exquisite message of existence.
We see beyond the radioactive putrescence.

We stay! Man must live on, and the song too must live on, for the heart
of the Universe shall break when the song ceases. I shall be the Orpheus
of the new life, and with my lyre I shall sing the dead out of the ground,
and with my words dispel death's clouds. We have not been expelled
from Paradise. With my song I shall domesticate the creatures of life
beyond death, and quieten the maddened machines. We shall beget
a child and seek out a bare field and we shall dig and there sow seed. We
shall be the new primeval parents of Mankind, wiser fathers and mothers
of the peoples to come, and we shall beget also new laws. Beget them,
and care for them. Beget and watch over them. And we shall tell the new
Mankind of what has been, and teach them the future. We are not
defeated: for greater than death is love. At love's flame-pyre we shall
watch on through the grim night without Mankind, and shall gather
around us the monsters, the chimeras, and the flowers.

NARRATOR

And the wreckage of Mankind enter the machine that had come down
from the Universe. And the jelly-armed butterfly-machine-beings
vanish after them in the machine's belly. And with a surge of blissful
bird-music, the disked metal sphere leaps up. And disappears into the
infinite.

The poet lets go his beloved's hand, looks about him, and sees amid the
ruins and bones the winds of gold-grey dawn leafing through dragonfly-

membranous wings of a book. He picks it up, and starts to read the lines
of verse aloud. Then, his arm around his beloved, he sets out in the
strange morning light towards the centre of the destroyed-green death-
paved desert of the world.

CHILDREN'S CHOIR

The day breaks.
A gold porcupine crawls up in space, pink nose seeking the way.

MEN'S CHORUS

The day breaks. Rest now, poet! Day breaks!
From your brain, perhaps, the gangrenous vision has withered
away.

CHORUS

The day breaks.
You are a seven-legged winged colt. On your back you bring
the Sun and the Moon.
Shake off the wasted years of dumbness. Begin then your
world-redeeming song.
Water your winged colts that through the Cosmos roam.
For your chest's gold fleece, your greasy skull-shock of hair
will turn grey soon!

POET

The day breaks. Gold tiles are roofing over darkness.
On my wakeful window I watch ruby-flecks falling.
Across my room's mauve wall, like X-rayed lungs' veiny lace,

light has printed the bushy cells of curtaining.
My lamp, like old soldiers' graveyards, grows fainter.
It gives no light—why should it?—to the light coming.
On my wife's neck, fluffy light-fields gleam brighter,
like star-clusters: shimmering, pulsing, paling.
Green boughs now falteringly pierce the night:
the joy-drunk nesting birds flutter, hover, raise and dip their
                        heads again,
they keep up a screeching, drink dew, hunt beetles.
And slowly the Sun waves across space his invincible
                        flag of Flame.


FULL CHORUS


*The day I wrote this the skies were clear,*
*And green boughs blossomed from the crags of Earth.*


POET


I believe in you, Mankind.
My imagined dead shall not defeat you.

                       [1964]

# Power
# of the
# flowers

O Rose and Hyacinth, Honeysuckle and Peony,
half-awake you sway in moonlight's lakes of mercury,
you moon peeling upon islands of light, fugitive slim Poppy,
face bloodied with rest, sleep oozes in you mysteriously,
like mothers standing at open windows, their bellies swollen,
becoming aware of teeth and eyeballs forming within them,
crying softly as they sway, dew on the dragging soreness,
a bright salt-fall in the moonlight upon weighted white breasts,
so you, trembling tall flowers, stand here in silence,
while the sphere of space powders your heads with yellow phosphorus.
In the steaming mooncake's white glimmer there dreams a Narcissus
like a thought on its long stem, in evening's stunned dusk,
you concepts, flowering out of slow speculation's soils,
love's embraces, shadowed kisses upon close bedside walls,
dear thoughts, wrung from a first metallic wince of worry,
sweet-smelling womb by wings enfolded flutteringly,
are you also to be found upon other planets circling by
and back again into unfathomable distance, upon star-larvae

in their meadows bathed by chrome sprays, cells steaming, your breath
clouding under foreign moons, with sticky armpits, because our earth
is but one among the Milky Way's thinning forests of blood-vessels

stretching

far out, do you sense the spine's vertebral keel of blind being,
and if a new bone should form, roadside sad wanderers, in time's

conical tail,

will you appear there too, who, arriving last, have yet not travelled at all?
Do you exist there, in some blissful place where no man nor beast is heard,
in some newly exploded or for a million years formless desert,
among red glues which the cooling striated matter secretes,
your fragrance singing among the columnar scaly pre-human beasts?
Are you trembling, as the rough pine-forests sough with choking

wind-snot, why

should you not shiver at the beaked shrieks from the feathered bird's

eye-covering sky,

fairy eyes, angel hands, tiny calf-mouths, ears of babies,
Moonflower, Hyacinth, Evening Primrose, Sweet Scabious?
Time's ears register sounds from space, on drawn threads of tin
silvered cups pick up voices and vibrate under the moon,
you are beyond understanding, miracles shrivelling and renascent,
Sweet Violets, boneless bodied, green-spined dreams with brains of scent,
bells of silence, one-legged secrets, lungs laid bare,
red kidney tissue, mute voices, who outlive time there,
yet you may not speak of those things which are your living secrets
through pollen-hoarse cords transformed into plant-glands in your

throats.

Are you to live only here, doomed to earth, to life exiled,
sentenced to beauty, with roots through this soil's tissue nailed,
to live only here, nowhere else, upon no other star nor planet,
with these waters swollen, dropsical, and with viscous fluids matted,
inhaling fire from a sun that sets system to atoms of the Milky Way,

like gold images your clustered stamens' facets catch its flames gloriously,
under only this rainbow-scarfed and flowerless moon,
like thoughts nowhere else to be found, nowhere else to be born?
O Rose and Hyacinth, Convolvulus and Celandine,
honey-thick flowers flowing over moonlit fields, releasing fine
scents in the slowly fuming lakes of air, why do
I feel my heart aching so, when I listen to you?
A homeland is what you are to me, no other earth I know
but this one, sour, white alkaline, nourishing black loam,
I cannot know whether your petals open ribbed baskets upon other
foreign planets; are such flowers there, Cornflower, Wisteria,
Musk Rose, Horned Poppy, Autumn Snowflake, Verbena,
Rock Rose, Convolvulus, Wild Fire Iris, Magnolia?
I cannot know, faithful ones, whether you are found in other soils,
do you light up beside hot waters, ignite where the sun's surface boils,
or faithfully only here push up leaves, wordless petals, stalks,
again and again, this earth's loyal children, cuddling her plains, her
                                                gentle hillocks?
Tiny mauve umbrellas, mute-tongued bells, soft dreaming towers
                                                of bloom,
from boughs hang blown flower-skulls, wax-petalled jugs with
                                                inscriptions of perfume,
stars of dust, treelets of mica, smooth veined petal-eyeballs,
foam-ribbed green candles, bloody beadings, straining projectiles,
along the roadsides you swallow dustclouds whitening the ditches,
there you burn on, in the grinding roar and through the silences,
as granite sifts over stone-breaking machinery's gears and grooves,
your outlines blur beneath fine dusts speeding from tires and hooves,
only the dew washes your faces, and the day's light rains
moisten ragged sun-dried foliage, hair-patterned veins,
through steam, sparks, soot, you push up along the railway-cutting,
on cinder-rivered trackbeds between sleepers and rails on tiptoe standing,

out on lakes of pitch and oil you swim, blue swans, heron-like plants,
yellow-headed, ochre-skulled, patiently surfacing at last,
firmly braced, metal-foliaged, pliable-skeletoned, whom courage stays,
when a slow freight-train rumbles by the milk-boned flesh tugs and
sways,
O virgins, breaking forth into the light, from the sharp black froth of
slag-heaps,
nymphs of the garbage, who can know anything of your joy's secrets?
You break out between the rags, the splintered glass, through rusted pots,
you are cradled, as if by floes, upon oceans of filth like white sailboats,
in crannies of newsprint, among pondweed-tangled metal shavings,
wires turning brown,
you grow like living coral, starry-fleshed chandeliers, in an Eden sea-garden,
you live on like insouciant immortals, or those resigned to being mortal,
thorny stemmed or star-strewing beauties, a flower-cup's fleshy handle
pushing up through dead cats' fragmenting rank liquefying flesh,
breaking through death upon his rotting throne of phosphorescence,
studded with pale-blue shells, the wrecked galleons of mouse skeletons
and gill-petals agitate the light, flames spinning from green fins,
you light up with the candles in cemeteries down overgrown side roads
like small yellow nightlights set over the meadow-abandoned dead,
beside soldiers' snail-house wax ears, blue wounded hearts of Uhlans,
from grandfathers' beards, upon shallow graves, sprouting from stillborn
babes' white palms,
like green wax-candles you light up in the red deer's hoofmark
who bares small teeth like round corncob-rows to strip young bark,
even on the dunghill among the pigs feet, chicken skulls, and frayed hooves,
on black iron bough-work, and fishscale-shingled sagging hutch roofs,
in the dragonfly-nosed wrecked airplanes' instrument-panels' earth-caked
dials,
in oily rubber-smelling membrane wings, where scorched aluminum curls,

your phosphorus-green growth encrusts pearled keels of green-slimy
sunken ships,
from the whitefish killed by pressure you creep forth from crumbling
fin-tips,
on islands of rotting fish-heads, cannon-shells, on doom-bombs' fins,
burning among brass cartridge-cases' lead-cored copper-sheathed organs,
your red lamps light up, and your white faces blink on again,
under the hairy flapping horse-carcass, where the light streams in
you stain the watery taut veins, and split the long bones' dry
pillars with white tortures, you ignite as you leap at the sky,
you ascend, like the revolving evening star, wet with tears, solitary,
you ascend, you shine resplendent in unutterable purity,
you ascend, green spirits, on green wings that beat up from the dust,
you ascend, your white glory unfolding, with radiant acceptance,
you ascend, skulls splitting, the black and yellow brains laid bare,
you ascend, from opened heads grow hearts of peace and also anger.
O Rose and Hyacinth, Narcissus and Fire-Tail,
sinless ones, that our hearts are less kind I know well,
such robust and mighty ones, who are brought forth in silence,
you know how to die without a word, lovers of meek yet heroic stance,
so many sins we carry, desire, selfishness, self-delusion,
saddened by suffering, indifferent through vanity, felled by resignation,
for we are but human, the substance we share is the same,
birth is a cry, and death a cry, and life a cry of pain.
The animals yelp also, panting they spill out their young in lairs,
to hatch her speckled eggs the small robin flushes with fevers,
the woman wails, screams, curses, heaving herself up like froth
before the bloodied brown infant's crown squeezes from her sheath,
and the child too is hurt, by the more than beautiful fearful combat,
pain turns it blue as a fish, screeching in slime, in blood, in fat,
in my last throes my body with dense cold pearls is studded,
I lie hardening into an idol of obsidian upon my bed,

but you flowers, who are pregnant with time, yet lack tongue
and protective skin, nerves of the earth, what makes you so strong?
You come suddenly as love, and pass like sorrow from where once you
                                                              stood,
simple-minded almost, intuition brims your chalices of solitude,
upon the thin brows of poor grazing lands, in the reaper's apron
you nod for the last time in the light, slim-legged, as he passes on,
blue veins start out of your calves, wings sprout at earth level,
                                                       snake-clawed
dreaming there and dreaming on, knotty-backed, bloated treefrog leaved,
tongues clubrooted, tongues purple, tongues in pollen-floured mouths,
                                              tongues like tridents,
flowers beheaded, six pendant petals like wry earlobes, a torso's desire
                                         speaking from bell-trumpets,
upon the quaking bog's clayey skin, where waterlogged feathergrass
                                                     grows green,
in the loose slides of shale upon hillsides, where grey falls of scree careen,
on the fine soils' creamy surface, where dry wrack withers between
                                                   extruded roots,
on the wilted, grey-tufted alkaline earths, on the long limbs of exposed
                                                            salts,
you brood on the slow brooks' spongy banks, green-scaled golden-headed
                                                     river nymphs,
and on the sour mountain pasture, the long ridged prairie's lips,
you are the earth's vocal cords, bulbs of honeyed salivas, with spinal
                                            columns of fish,
soft teeth of living tissue for the neck's nape, bladders for ears, foreheads
                                                 growing fins,
in the tangles of underbrush, underneath rotting treetrunks and
                                                      toadstools,
upon pale circles of limestone rubble, covered with shell eggs of frail
                                                            snails,

you silent fairy-named flowers close-knotted to my heart,
Christ's Glove, Baby's Breath, Blue-Eyed Mary, Sweet Violet.
Here you flame up in me, mute souls of my earth, joy and sorrow,
Snowball Rose, White Wings Rose, Christmas Rose, Meadow Rue,
your roots pass around my heart, into my broken soil you enter,
for I am this Earth that reared you, I your mother, your prisoner,
nor would I be myself without you, I who sent you out to live,
bald wastelands would poison me, but you live on because in you I
                                        believe.
I would stare blindly into the void, if metals and minerals covered my
                                        surface,
if barren coloured dusts coated my face, what would be my purpose?
Here glimmer the star-like head, green stalk, blue window of your body,
Lady's Mantle, Crimson Flag, Pearl Bush, Blue Rosemary,
here you dwell in me, Snowdrop, Winter's Sexton, Autumn Snowflake,
Sweet Cornflower, Marsh Marigold, Fire Thorn, and Tamarisk.
O you dispellers of sorrow, magic-named wordless breathing wonders:
Love Lies Bleeding, Love-in-a-Mist, Orange Heliopsis, Everlasting
                                        Flowers,
Bishop's Hat, Lords and Ladies, Black-Eyed Susan, Blue-Eyed Mary,
Golden Rod, Blue-Eyed Grass, Yellow Gorse, Blue Holly,
Bears' Ears Primula, Leopard's Bane, Peasant's Eye Narcissus, Hound's
                                        Tongue,
Horned Poppy, Opium Poppy, Iceland Poppy, Wallflower Fire King.
And all of you whom I have not called upon, whom I do not name, mate
upon my summits, on my high pasture, in my lowlands you vibrate,
striking root overnight, breaking time's close-mouth rock with quiet
                                        insistence,
bringing with you sweetly sorrowful yet joyous scent of pristine existence,
you, born in the settling still-warm muds, after the first blow of creation,
little sisters of the metals, and salts' daughters born in cosmic copulation,

you starry breasts of radiance, bird-form constellations, spiral nebulae
                                        of the snails,
voracious progeny at the nipples of the elements, who sink down slow
                                        black nails,
you green calves suckling at the teats of phosphorus, copper, boron,
                                        sulphur, iron,
salts' ganglions, kin to volcanoes, feathers ruffling along beds of silicon,
you dreams of nitrogen, whose kiss burned off the last particles of metal
                            when you left the womb of gold,
procreations of flame, embryos of creative mists, messages such as
                            shifting rainbows hold,
you materialize from vapors dense as hot aluminum, you are the germinal
                                        desires
of blue rainfalls, the incubated spinal cells of the sun's centre fires,
green slimes, membranous goiters, heart-hatted necks, grand-children of
                                        conflagrations,
growing out of the blood-coloured, the yellow, the blue-black bottle-green
                            rocks, your relations,
you slight womanish brothers of the thundering oceans, primeval
                            mothers of greasy whale herds,
infant twins of crabs, of long-necked ocean-cleaving finned things and
                            wading tall birds,
sisters to fishes and dragons, lizards' great-grandfathers,
cousins of snakes, birds' forebears, insects' elder brothers!
You are the future of the fires of metals, iron semen seethes in your
                                        hormones,
mothers of oils, coal's genitalia, redeeming heralds of bones,
you flowers have travelled through measureless time and space
on frail green-shod feet, rooted always in one and the same place!
O flowers, nothing is unknown to you, flowers of my land,
through your cells there is howling still the primeval wind,
it roars through the inner rooms of protons and neutrons,

proclaiming the blessedness of birth in their starry constellations,
it blows across the frontiers of fire and procreation, through the scented
> silence,
and your milliard heads sigh together, touching in bliss, in loneliness,
gold godheads are blown forth from your wombs, creatures of fine meal,
and your open love was covered by a flowing yellow veil,
flowers, who have lived through the past, what know you of me,
what do you know of my heart, why it lives so avidly,
why proud faith is beautiful, why I find pain in the rain showers,
why my consciousness puts forth heavy-scented, undyingly fair flowers?
Flowers, timeless ones, yet easily broken as I have seen,
with narrowing leaves for shoulders, hips of gelatine,
gland-browed, lips growing from larynx, and tenderness in your thorns,
my flowers, fragile dreams, pliant-ribbed, spear leafed ones,
my flowers, black tongued, gold collared, milk within you for blood
> circulating,
my flowers, bald lunged, tallow skulled, from a corpse's armpit growing,
my flowers, flat your close hair, your adam's apples with shell ribbing,
mealy vocal cords from the open-wound larynx like clappers hanging,
my flowers, watery fleshed, with milk at the waist sagging,
what shall man do, when he is left to himself, and his dreaming?
My flowers, I call on you conquering ones, and say that man must still
> dream on,
you must never fall, for only thus will he be able to remain human!
Live on, you green instincts, unfold into the young air
your resplendent lip-cups, on wide-arching pillars of green hair,
like parachutes opening out into each other in series
slung from the male body, their chain falling across space,
so you float across the million years' plain, opening and re-opening,
on and on, umbel, stalk, tuber eternally opening, eternally floating.
You have heard the seething of a tremendous sea which never knew
> jellyfish, crab, nor stingray,

and have seen the towering jets of whales disporting in the moonlit
bland bay,
and how the yellow-finned, pole-necked, mouse-toothed Plesiosaurians,
the swimming mammal lizards, kissed the purple sea-anemones in the
oceans,
seen the stranded rose-headed squids upon the sands drying out to glass,
how soft red bellies of the cactus-armoured reptiles touch in gentle
dalliance,
back and forth swinging between shell-covered thighs, the soft-veined
onion-clapper
in the blue furry nest, and glass-brittle melonballs in the lined sac move
and quiver.
You saw the armoured Gigantosaurus' bloody battles,
the rending jaws of chrome green, thorn-crested reptiles,
how the Tri-Corn pushed his bone pike far into the breast of the Lizard
King,
whose yellow-purple lung-clots and fats welled out with the flood of
blood mingling,
the swish of the first birds on squealing wings, the awkward
roaring also of turtle-sized beetles you heard,
you felt the procreating storms of love-symbol marked moths of great size,
you saw the painful slow trek of the turtles, heard their death sighs,
you felt the wind of man's flashing metal arrow,
you saw the pursed sweet smile of the Avar baby, and long ago
the Huns' rushing cloud of horse, huge-chested whirlwind of a thousand
nostrils,
in your dew the Thracian virgin washed her blood-gummed nipples,
a love-sick Latin maiden gazed up from where she lay at the axes of your
petals,
and you set upon the gypsy's nose, when he bent over you, a yellow
pimple,

you heard the bellowing of bullocks when from the dust-cloud they
raised
the Magyars swooped, harrassed behind, longing for the beeches' shade,
in that wanderers' apocalypse, the battle-axes, death rattles,
wailings, and spears, are preserved in your parts with the great lost
battles,
iron flowers of silence, glass-tongued flowering clubs, grasses like wires,
you have preserved the possible conceiving of curses, kisses, prairie-fires,
and the dust-veiled dirge of every ragged devout procession
that carries the green-stone form nailed onto wood, the Second Person,
you hold the wilted suffering of all guilty rebels,
the mail-clad stallions' grey-green lips of rheumy piles,
beneath the passing shadowed roar of the bomber each of you trembles,
collapsing stone-woods, burning blood bubble-sprays stain your petals,
you have heard the soft addresses of stern poets,
life-giving mothers' ecstatic screams, cursings of prophets,
flowers, crucibles of scent, in the moonlight here trembling,
shining like money, like divination, tender shadows throwing,
oh in the steaming mooncake's white glimmer, the brooding Narcissus
blooms beside sleeping saurians and blue lizards,
I hardly know whether small moths or petals, mongrel-descendants,
are flooding the little brook with quicksilver blue radiance,
under films of nickel the in-motion for eternity sleeping foliage floats,
in and out dance the tiny scintillating fishes with pulsing white throats.
I know only this, that I am human and from instincts of seaweed,
hot primeval muds, mortal and eternal, I have risen indeed,
consciousness purified in flame, a cell arrived at man's estate;
I do not know, world, your ways, but I manage, I estimate
what is to be done with courage and as you, world, would have it done,
this you can in no way understand, Violet, Viburnum.
You can in no way understand that what is brought through me to
blossom among us

is a flower that can speak, and is fairer far than the moonlight Narcissus,
its stalk grows up towards space, giving its scent to time's future,
meteoric time dusts its stamens, its petal's root will not wither,
thinking back to the first cleaving evokes pain and impurity in turn,
I carry within me the scales, dragon-crests, gills, fins, skin,
feathers, star-mists, seas, plants, fires, iron, lime, sand,
oh this, flowers in the moonlight trembling, you in no way understand!
You do not fathom it, Iris and Rue, though you outlive me,
Rose and Hyacinth, Honeysuckle and Peony.

[1955]

# The grave of
# Attila József

*Though in my lifetime I trod among thorns,*
*I shall rot beneath roses when the time comes ;*
*In the Kerepes Cemetery*
*My grave shall overflow with flowers.*

Gyula Reviczky

Rose of imagination, thought's narcissus, mind chrysanthemum, lily of
                                                        nothing,
fermenting, raving, heavy-mouthed, piled blind flowers with teeth of scent,
heaped lily, narcissus, rose, fragrant-brained silence upon your puny
                                            grave, your paltry
child's grave, my Master, my Brother, my Ancestor, my Father,
                                        my Jesus-genitalled very
own dead, frail stallion of the universe, angel-winged blue crystal,
whimpering web of life's nervous system, you orphaned small boy
                                    heading the columns of the dead,
galaxy-foreheaded, weeping at world-black pain of brother for lost
                                        brother, fine scalpel
grafting a new lens upon God's cataracting eye, world's
sliced eyeball which grows over again like the crested newt's

on excision: in the brain-box bulges spongy fresh fungus, fruit of the will,
dragon-pupilled, flower of living glass; on your child-sized grave
green epics, summergold bone-brittle statues of nettles, holly, Christ's
thorn-tree,
crinkled electric light, flaking tin-cans, standing rainwater in gloom
the rising tears of the dead, congealed veins around last year's candle-end,
black the
worm of its Holy Ghost spine, the pink discharge of last year's candle
which
we burnt with Erzsike pondering my fate, and yours pondering.


For you lie here on the other side of the road, here your heart rotted open,
here your brain seeped away, through the light skull's broken bubble of
bone,
like the gristle oozing shorewards within its freshwater clam, from the
brain-box draining
away like rose-brown soap from the cracked-apart lye crock,
here your mind became the white impulse of white maggots, of snowy
lime-caked larvae, here
lie your bones within the black earth's folds in anguished scrawls
like the first scratched characters in my small daughter's book, you
First Writing, First Symbol,
Idea's Ignition, Arc of Beginning, Straight Course Thereafter. First
Flexing, Child's Scribble on God's heart, nervously I stand where you
lie six feet down
on the other side of the road, below brave roses of imagination
in this paltry grave, with mould covered over like a lime-strewn
execution yard, you lie with one shoulderblade wrenched from its
flower-socket
of red flesh, dusk wore you as a bloody shirt, Flower threaded by a
railway wheel,

you suffuse the staring eyeball of immense evening, here in this smallish
                                   littered and weed-grown grave,
where like faces of dead tramps, rubber profiles of imbeciles, the snails
                                                   swell and slobber,
the sweet and hot and sombre summer crackles into flame, with
                               somewhere a harp, cymbals, a violin,
fire ascending, crickets and grasshoppers poised like gothic, beetles
                                                   grapple mating,
and stuck-fast paired dragonflies flit like pendulant diamonds past this
                                                   puny grave,
ragged like the fur of run-over dogs, broken whiskers of starting-eyed
                                                   dead cats,
and I keep looking at the withered, cracked green-spotted toad which
has eaten of you, even as I in my childhood have eaten of the body of
                                                   God.


For you lie here on the other side of the road, in this paltry proletarian
                                                   grave,
in this capitalist filth of stone, bronze, and granite, this abomination,
this raving money-paradise, among bumptious bronze manufacturers,
dim fathers in marble, stocky mares strung around with white marble
                                                   roses,
here heavy-helmeted imbecile gentry generals, there meditative
bronze hunters cradling yellow shotguns, their bronze hats and
                               moustachios inclining
to the shit that rains down from pigeons, wrens, woodpeckers, blackbirds,
                                                   you lie here
among the whores dreamed up in marble, pumice shifts modelling the
                                                   aristocratic arses
of poorly endowed young ladies, marble angels' wings spread to the dawn,
hair falls forward upon chests of Jesuschrists, black marble

for captains of industry, half-witted stone counts, shiny medalled
nitwit Army officers, brooding princes of commerce pouchy in bronze,
granite-bellied bankers, well-born young men heavenwards aspiring,
marble sons of industrialists in Apollo get-up, their faces
blackened with bands of mourning worn by
rainwater flowing from empty eyesockets, here you lie lonely
on the other side of the road, and nearby the blessed bones, those that
                                       were cursed, of Leda,
here you lie among bronze-edged granite lids, a river of pack-ice
                                             riding up
block frozen to jumbled block, marble undercut to froth,
among stone hearts of the Virgin with seven daggers through them,
bronze horses shade you with hard waves of moulded mane, the hot
                                      bronze stallions whose
pendulous balls were not torn off by grenades, here you lie
                                    in weed-choked, parched,
cinder-dry, tearless, deathless, life-rejecting, coldly glittering, ultimately
dead capitalism, in the vertigo of half-bared nipples of
stone virgins; that epileptic devil, Dostoevsky's Satan,
spewed up this cemetery all over the world, Mammon's cow sick at last
on champagne and women—or bull, Mammon's bull threw up and there
                                    was this graveyard,
last resting-place of your bones, and Reviczky's, and Babits', and Ady's,
                                    and Arany's,
and Vajda's, and the bones of Móricz, Kosztolányi, Lajos Nagy; so the
                                    cemetery became
a cup of earth holding your heart, a second womb, You Who Are Dispersed,
Embryo of the Universe, Immortal Forefather, Born yet Hardly
Born yet—if I scratched through to you with my teeth, my nails,
dug down to you with my eyes, I would find nothing left of your
                                    bloodied smile,

nothing left of your velvet throat, nothing left of your boyish brow,
only bones, bones, bones, bones, bones, yellow bones
and rotted tatters of clothes.


For you lie here on the other side of the road, and there is no god near you
and there is no man near, only Leda's strong limbs, only Leda's
world-lulling womb slowly powdering to putrescence between the
                                                    unopenable
chiselled Bible, pressed petals in a prayerbook, she will never rustle forth
filling out the full flower of flesh, with the glass shiver of her wild mare's
                                                    snicker
for resurrection was not for such as her, only to continue, and she
does not rise out of the earth, mauve mane hanging loose to wipe from
                                        her thighs the mould,
coffin-wood flecks, and root-bored dust, to the Last Judgement's
ineffable red storm trumpets, star-spraying angels' trumpets,
and only she rotting away close to you, not Vörösmarty, not Arany,
and not the little cottonwool figure, our old red Santa of December,
                                        Old Jókai,
only you lie here on the other side of the road, the Most Foresaken,
                                        Most Lonely,
Taunter, Indicter, Weigher upon Consciences, you lie here on the other
                                        side
of the road, under my heedless, triumphing, anguished, world-flowering
summer heartbeats; huge my black gaze that searches the earth,
probing the planet's deposits, twin searchlights in the terrified
night of summer, where I see your body-metal glinting, like wings
of an aircraft, its fuselage, astral dome, armoured skins
in the rhinoceros thunder of space, and I see: in your teeth the yellowing

fillings of blue slate, little gold-rooted trees, undying candleflame, tawdry
made on credit subterranean molar crowns, gold circlets for the
skull-castled
bone princes, underground flames, petrified goldfish, rough-barked
small trees, gold-clawed tiny primeval wrinkled crabs, their feelers ringed
with years,
I can make out the molybdenum stars of your poverty, your mouth's fires
deep down under
its stiffened volcano-wings, I see fingers that never wore a ring, only God
marked you,
Bird no man ever ringed, Most Beautiful White Crane, unique the
fuzing sperm, unique the egg from which only you could come, by a
unique bird breast warmed,
only you could knit star to star with your dipping flight, Spider-god
linking with gold web the echoing spaces, I see your hairless face of bone,
your engaging white grin, and I see, Poor One, insane use
of wealth scattered throughout earth's layers, underground chambers
leased and
freehold, gilt-rimmed glasses, halls plated with squared marble,
metal moisture-proof coffins, gilded chests gigantic upon lion paws,
and I see the mould-stained silk-weighty shrouds, gold threaded
orgies of lace, and all that sickening fairytale of tailcoats and morning
dress, armour and ballgowns,
pelisses, red leather boots, gold bells and gold spurs, flowered
headdresses,
cuirasses, metal-framed ornaments, ornate mother-of-pearled gloves,
and bow-ties, top-hats, goldcloth waistcoats, fragrant bonnets,
embroidered aprons,
buttonboots and suede slippers from the repellent world of Grimm,
gold braid peeling away from topboots, in glass slippers bone toe-pieces
with silvered toe-nails; these I see and you, Proletarian of the Dead,

as with a deep-probing telescope trained at the faint galaxies' luminous
pale skytrails and starry chains of radiant gold, I see you defrauded,
made mad, raving, driven to kneel to the freight train,
and I see gold, in rings, in diamond pins, in rows of dull metal teeth
                                                                    jutting
up like squat corncobs from underground, jagged, deathly,
in the haze of restructured matter's pale gold beard, I see a people's
                                            blood frozen in slow gold,
gulped from fisted chalices, I see gold brooches thick as a man's prick,
buckles under the sea of roots, and like gold sunflowers the crests
                                                            surmounting
helmets, swordhilts, rapier blades double-grooved for blood,
gold watches protruding like rounded bone ends, gold laurel wreathes
                                                upon disintegrating
skulls with brains of earth, like dried-up fishscales,
on fingers of bone I see gemmed rings mount guard over time,
like magnified eight-eyed spiders' heads, diamond bracelets rotate
on flaring lace-fringed sleeves caught in at bone wrists,
like bands of colour blinding a child who stares at the sun;
I see you who will never decay, you unwilting wreath of stars, from this
                                                                    side
and from the other side of the road, this and the other side
of the sea, scattered at random across this planet, underwater in green
                                                seaweedy bundles
studded with plants and shells, and at the water's edge bundles with
                                    feathery yellow roots wrapped,
grown-over with lime-crystal flowers in tall calcite patterns, I see how
the bodies ferment, exhale and liquefy, turn red, waxen-skinned,
their flesh swelling like marsh scum, organs bright as swamp flowers
squelch against bones, bones turning to quartz, this side of the sea
and on the other side of the road.

For you lie here on the other side of the road, there was none like you,
white diamond your structure, You Always Fearing Retribution, how
                                   scared you must be here by yourself,
for here also you are alone. At the last stop of loneliness, cosmic storms
fever my brain's corona, my thoughts' terrifying solar flares
lick at your disarranged bones, aren't you scared to lie here among such
                                                          wild beasts,
hyenas were these corpses once, a panther's those bones of some pearled
                                                       female, voracious
and given to bone crunching, aren't you afraid, dear One,
that the earth will haemorrhage, gasping for breath, its glowing bird's egg
                                                        centre splitting,
its yolk's skin tear open, flooding your bones with blood, blood, blood,
the earth's purple, heavy, thick blood, jetting as from a camel's
holed throat, blackly flows blood, blood, blood, are you not scared,
                                                            loved One,
that the fire's sprouting teeth of low flame will devour your skull,
the fire, fire, fire, fire from the earth's seams breaking, like love
that blasts forth from the earth's loving heart, broken in mourning,
like flame from open furnace doors, aren't you scared, lonely frightened
                                                                   One,
that fire, flame, blood will leap across the totalled aeons' crusted layers
                                                             of stars,
over fern forests, giant mammals, the flesh of amorous dragon fathers,
                                                        bird mothers,
over snail, crab, spider, dragonfly, fish, flowerseed, and that blood, fire,
                                                        blood will leap at
and consume your scattered bones?


For they lie there on the other side of the road, the angry, the
                                            magnificent companions,

all of them lonely, but all belonging together, huddled close
like blind young under a striped cat's moist mother belly, the new-born
nuzzling there
hungry for suck, sobbing together and sharing their fear,
for them playing cards and reciting verse is consolation enough and hope,
I can hear them under the earth slapping down the cards,
like the writhing of fish in a net, flat tails clapping,
floundering stiffly; and faintly through the earth I can hear Mihály
Babits,
chanting shamanic lines of verse, he was wronged, that miraculous one,
wearing his fear lightly there Kosztolányi chatters on, and smiling into his
dense moustache
is world-hearted Móricz, Lőrinc Szabó banging his fists
raises bone blisters, and János Vajda makes to run again
from a bone Gina, and Gyula Reviczky puts his arms around a Jászai
whom feathery roots embrace,
and Lajos Nagy is searching for you who are exiled, hounded from their
mould paradise,
and he drums with bone fingers on a bone table,
flapping tatters like vulture's wings, he sets the earth moving,
sinking, caving-in, seething, he flutters in the draught
bare ribs like a wing-frame as if to fly away, and he is bored.


Even here is no society, no companions for you, for you who weep,
no homeland, no smallholding, no graveyard back home, no blissful
death,
for you no parish churchyard sown with ancestors, only a box-width
at Szárszó, there death slipped you in with a collector's pitiable blunt
fingers, you
rarer than all Darius' treasures, a heavily thudding penny struck in iron,

poor small coin, its brain clouded with verdigris, with this you have
                                        paid Existence off,
and you tumbled into the ground's box a second time, poor One,
those words of your death paid for with the rusting coin of your heart,
you tumbled into this summery mouldy, flame-flowering small grave,
you firstborn among the dead, greatest of earth's poet-kings,
why, seven stars your right hand held at your birth, and
a double-edged sword cut its way out of your mouth, a sun your face,
dear Heart, when you died, halfway from heaven flew an angel
who said to the peoples of the earth, in a loud voice,
woe, woe, woe, and his words were spoken to three angels
who will be trumpeting yet.


For woe to us, woe to the earth, if with our star-dense words we cannot
steady the world's pivot, with words lark-wing light, or
words fire-trailed, words whale-spouting, or mastodon-heavy
lumbering words, or with words of velvety inner narcissus petals
seal shut the furnace at the white-hot world's core, and
with words soft as babies' soles pad your frail small body,
your soapbubble frail body taken down from the cross of the world
into the dank, icy-breathed and moisture greased
grave-box, and I thought, woe to me, some twelve years back,
twelve years ago exactly, woe to me who was sent after to follow you,
                                        fugitive,
tender you were, for an ultimate love yearning, an orphan calling upon
                                        God,
woe, woe, woe, you had cried and I too had kept crying, over your
                                        overgrown small autumn grave,
brown and dry like the wispy hairs at the loins and breasts of old
                                        people's corpses,

there I stood with Erzsike who was expecting a child, her belly a living
                                                                    egg,
there she stood with me, mother of the universe, and before your grave
                                                            she watched
my worker's hands, thin-skinned now, which from calloused bricklayers
                                                        had bloomed,
from day-labourers, cottagers, bondsmen forefathers all, over your
                                                    gnawed thin bones
she watched them pass: in her belly turns love's exquisite bubble,
a tiny gold-fisted star, its pearled knees protruding,
contracting and stretching like glistening soft snails' horns,
and its eyes shall roll open like the rock stopping Christ's cave tomb,
woe, let this pass from me, let me not suffer a fate like yours, may our
                                                                    fates
not be the like of yours, nor resignation our lot,
nor collapse, desolation, fear, escape,
nor her lot either whose mother egg swells, nor of the one about to come;
yet there in space was a huge red dragon with seven heads, ten horns,
seven crowns on his heads, his tail trailing a third part
of heaven's stars, and with these he lashed down at earth, and that
                                                                dragon
came close to the mother-to-be, and oh! I tried to grasp his throat,
sinuously elusive, dragonishly soft-flowing through my hands, and
                                                            flame-hot,
and he wrapped his seven towering necks round me,
belched his lungs' fire, smoked, spat out upon my wire-brush skull,
singeing my eyelashes, moustache, and I was a scorched sunflower,
then from out of your grave, shining like a greater dragon, your diamond
                                                                sword
arose, and I wrenched my diamond sword out of my heart and cut off
                                                    the dragon's heads,

the bare earth ran with blood hot from the spouting trunks,
the necks were tree-trunks seeping blood, stars turned red,
dragon's heads crashed upon more distant stars, filling space with the
                                                    sound of harps,
the dragon's tongues turned to mould like half-buried stone-boats,
jonquils and lilies bloomed in melon-sized jellied eye-sockets,
and I stood there before your autumn-dark grave, your earth-filled skull
cast a flickering light from the grave, warming my shivering heart, and
I kept rubbing my blood-wet hands, wiping the drying blood on the
                                                    nettles of your grave,
and I was no longer crying out and talking aloud, I only cursed you,
your accursed grandeur, invincible and beloved, and I cried
for you and I cried for the world and longed for a sweet graveyard at
                                                    home,
for a serene death, a cheerful resting-place.
For not even this was granted you, a graveyard at home,
You the Father of Completeness, yet lacking a resting-place within
                                                    yourself,
no sumach tree for you, no black-green elder, poplar, thorn-tree, nor
                                                    locust tree
grew from sweet shrivelled wombs of grandmothers, no elder sprouting
                                                    from the mighty
walrus-moustached ancestors, no bird-pulsing nesting place, no fluffy
tremulousness, no eggshells' blood-veined slippery emptiness scattering
                                                    upon you dried
sperm kernels, no moaning lovemaking in the white and purple chestnut
                                                    trees,
sweet their bone-melting scented sweetness, the armoured fluffy-faced
bee's crystal skull with eyes of seven thousand cells, the down to the
                                                    breastbone sunken
red tombstones with their graven green lichen-grown verses, the young
                                                    girls blistering

upon their photographs do not see you, black rain-gouged stone
                                    grandfathers
do not speak to you; nor like hens perched on a mulberry tree for the
                                    night
do grandmothers speak to you, nodding in the Death Tree's foliage
                    reaching down into the earth's centre,
sleepily clucking at the blood-swollen crest of the cock who lives there in
                                    the fire;
for you the whitewashed effigy Christs do not disrobe each spring
like gentle grass snakes, sloughing off with a moan brittle flakes of white
                                    skin
on flowing bloody May nights, when the shirts of whitewash flutter
                        from their shoulders,
their crusted white face-masks break into pieces in the swelling new
                                    grass, like
stars in the lake exploding from the glass heads of jumping fish, and it
                                    happens
that the inquisitive dead thrust up newly buried heads, like
ears of wheat, bone chests, armbones, and skulls starting from the ground;
you are not carried up in the graveyard which climbs aloft like a Gold
                            Griffin on All Souls Eve,
flying up into sounds reflected from space, a mighty bird blissfully
                                    circling
feathered with candleflames, Death's Table ready laid,
star-welded bier of grace, flame-leafed fragrant baytree
that overgrows the roof of space, sparkling and shining like the biblical
                                    glass lake,
that shines and blazes like trumpets in the seraphims' choir,
the gleaming jaw of St John's Apocalypse.

For you lie here on the other side of the road, yours was not to be even
that much
home, that much homeland, that much land,
You Spontaneous Pronouncer of the World, born joyfully to come into
the estate of the universe
but turned to aimless brooding in the territories of loneliness,
in the forests of sadness, with metal-heavy mulberry leaves on your
shoulder,
how you longed for the glades of childhood, if only you had been given
bones, black bones,
shiny bones to be laid across the heart, vertebrae threaded
like beads, jasper-eyed bone relatives, younger and older
bone brothers, bone grandfathers, bone forefathers and bone ancestresses;
you were not granted a Memory Tree in the love-sown tiny graveyard,
no shrouded deep Memory Tree, webbed with colours of rain, growing
down
to the running white iron planet's heart, putting down more
arboriferous veins through flesh into gold, gold to fire; and its crystal
moustached
ruby bearded and emerald haired naked fruits are all the young brothers,
little sisters,
grandchildren, elder sisters, and brothers, grandparents, ancestors, birds,
fishes, vermin
lodged in the Death Tree's stone-barked deep plunging broad branches,
in its measureless dense crown, sprouting from gold, like birds of
paradise
in death-stitched black plumaged gowns, white lace-veiled bundles
betrothed to death, like the flowering lace gloves drawn on by hands of
hoarfrost,
in topboots with silver moustache like the photo of János Arany when
young,

in strawberry pink mother-of-pearl buttoned bodice like my
                              grandmother of only thirty years,
in nests warmly lined with the living, they crowd the Death Tree's
                                                        branches
humming and chattering, twittering, singing, talking,
gaping coloured slant-vented beaks, and pecking off with
their jointed bills mint-scented leaves from the Death Tree,
from their glowing pelvises groan forth the eggs of all fairy tales, and
                                        the black speckled
death eggs are cracked open in spring by slim sea-horse heads of
sticky-flanked winged foals, seven-headed dragon chicks with
scales soft as babies' nails, diamond crowned snake princesses, little
                                                baby-handed
helpless frog kings, man-eating faery damsels
from whose mouths men's legs, men's feet, long-haired skulls protrude
as from a bolting chicken's neck maggots or caterpillars'
hairs, winged waterbeetles' green mulberry sacs, dragonflies'
brittle diamond-chandeliered heads, giant moths' chasuble-wings,
                                        grasshoppers'
red vein woven membrane-wings.


For not even this was given you, to die in serenity and
serenely to love, only this box in the earth here, and in four milliard
                                        human hearts
only here and there a grave-plot for you, loved One; but there's a bloody
                                writhing grave-plot
in each and every heart, loved One: in the vermin, the beetles, the larvae,
the birds, the fishes, the mammals, the lepidoptera,
all feathered things, the armadillos, silken-skinned creatures,
those with exteriorized skeletons, the invertebrates, and spider-bodied,

in the spiral snail-shaped, the bladder-propelled, the water mammals,
and the big cats, the amphibia, animals of the Zone of Cancer,
hairy swimming things, the hydra-headed, and the trees,
the grasses, the lichens, the mosses, the flowers and in the rocks,
in the water and in the flame, in the gaseous stars and in the heart of
                                                             creation.


For there was nothing else for you to inherit, uniquely Unique Man,
than four milliard graves, milliard milliard grave-pits writhing
at the heart of all that is, and your grave the cosmos itself, the milliard
milliard roots of existence, shredded and stiff, shifting and soft, fluid
and mineral; from plants and animals love-milk roots tap your heart,
you Proletarian Nobody, the Universe sprouted from your heart, Life
                                                             and Death,
you gutted Rose rooted in Freud's heart, bravest of all,
you Coward who gave up, because you could not put the world's
                                                   splintered glass ball
together again, and the world's crystal supports crashed
down, and you are lying beneath them like a mammoth
in primeval ice, with the hide of your being intact, your heart's amethyst
                                                             incisors,
for you sold out to death, you have dissolved like sugar
in the liquid of life, and your sighs rose in bubbling twigs through it of
                                                             blood,
and you are everywhere and you are nowhere at all.


Where shall I seek you, for I thirst greatly, for I am all alone,
I with no drink, I who need you as brother needs brother,
for I need you to hurt and to love me, you who from a thousand milliard cells
built Tense Awareness, you Easter cell-church of blissfulness,

for I have to hit out at you, and need to feel always your blow to my
                                                                    heart,
hear your voice crying out with mine, as the child with his father, for fathers
                                                                    do not
run away in front of their sons, and I hate those who escape;
and where am I to seek you, for I thirst, I am parched
so that I am dry hair and nothing else, and within nothing but hair and
                                                                    bones
and eyeballs, I sit on the barren island of song and wait for you as
those shipwrecked wait for the big fish, they carve a hole in the big
                                                                    fish's side
and watch it fill up slowly with clear lymphatic fluid,
and dipping cracked mouths into the fish's body they sip,
gulping down with throats of porcelain the fish's juices.
But where are you my Fish, Saviour Fish, that I may cut a hole
through to your heart, and suck out oily redolent juices,
and have my monster-teeming night pass from me?


For you are nowhere and you lie here on the other side of the road,
in a small proletarian grave in this rich man's flaunting, tricked-out
infamous showpiece, this marble, metal, granite, bronze-
vomit, in this Garden of Sins, this Land of Lies,
for you there was no balsam, no golden body-sheath, no stiff painted
                                                                    gown,
no granite coffin, underground death palace, no god-mourners
as for Egypt's kings, crocodiles, bird gods,
nor goldleaf headpiece wrought in the form of leopard, tuna, squid,
                                                                    or peacock
for kingly brow, on your face no beaten-gold mask, soft as grasshopper's
                                                                    skin,
to protect the features' crater-life, record the face's cell-system

and preserve the lashes of lids closing decayed eyes
like gold-filament lace collars, that would preserve
the instant of murder, the smile of annihilation,
the empty desert of hair tufts as for Agamemnon;
for you there was no balsam, no gold, no god-mourners,
you lie like a flaking log, glistening in a web of roots and a borrowed suit,
you of the Ripped-away Sleeve, your forehead marked with train-wheel

rust,

and you lie here in this small proletarian grave, you Unassimilable,
for the earth can never disintegrate you, the earth's gloom-throated shark,
that steel-blue marked savage straining on the line, in whose opened belly
roll the swordfish heads, thorn-braceleted sea-cucumbers, half-gnawed
children's skeletons, and sea-stars' bony crowns in the stomach's juices,
in the grave's stomach like a sea-star's thorn-rose sprawls
your unassimilable skeleton, you Steadfast One, and in my heart lie
your unresolvable sea-star's crown verses;
and I reach down for you, for I have the power to do so,
I lift you from the root-fibres' shroud, and take you on my lap
like a male Madonna and with my streaky hair I wipe your bones,
with my tears wash your yellow bones, and rock in my arms
your skull washed in my blood, freed from its sinews,
and I weep and weep and weep and weep and cover with kisses
your indissoluble bones.

[1963]

# The works of Ferenc Juhász

## POETRY

1949 *Szárnyas csikó 1946–49* (The Winged Colt)

1950 *A Sántha család* (The Sántha Family)

1950 *Apám* (My Father)

1951 *Új versek* (New Poems)

1953 *Óda a repüléshez* (Ode to Flying)

1954 *A nap és a hold elrablása* (Laying Hold of the Sun and the Moon)

1954 *A tékozló ország* (The Spendthrift Country)

1955 *A virágok hatalma* (Power of the Flowers)

1957 *A tenyészet országa. Összegyűjtött versek 1946–1956* (The Breeding Country: Collected Poems 1946–1956) 720 pp.

1965 *Virágzó világfa. Válogatott versek 1946–1964* (The Flowering World Tree. Selected Poems 1946–1964) 417 pp.

1965 *Harc a fehér báránnyal* (Battling the White Lamb)

1969 *A szent tűzözön regéi* (Legends of the Holy Flood of Fire) 460 pp.

## PROSE

1967 *Mit tehet a költő?* (What the Poet Can Do) 223 pp.